It's My Fault

By: A.D. Whittington

Lanette 'Lyn' Hayes

Thanks for always being a true friend

4/26/85 – 9/17/11

The End.....
of life as you know it.

"Sometimes we don't want to hear the truth but once it's processed, it makes sense for the balance of life."

A.D. Whittington

Well hello, I finally wrote a book for you all. Folks have been asking me for quite some time about my words being transferred to this form (for those that need a break down, people kept asking me when I was going to write a book). I finally took the steps to make it happen which just involved sitting down to organize my thoughts and make sense of it all when I typed everything together. Pretty simple, but I was my own obstacle and I am definitely the core inspiration to touch your soul. I know I moved rather slowly, but I finally realized that honest insight is needed for the world to truly grow.

This isn't a novel but it's not a bunch of rambling that will make you feel like you can never reach what you keep hearing you should strive for. You know, a 'get- healed-quick-and-your-troubles-will-disappear-simply-because-you're-reading-these-words' type of magic folks like to expect when they buy a book instead of doing solid evaluations of who they really are. This isn't instant gratification without a whole lot of effort on your part, actually all the effort has to come from you. This book is not written in traditional form or what the critics will think displays "perfect presentation", but you will be able to understand exactly how I view life and relate it to your world on some level. Even if you aren't perfect with grammar or striving to be an entrepreneur someday, you deserve support with growing in a positive direction. I am so blessed that I can relate to any and everybody, regardless of the background. I have gone through so many things to gain personal knowledge and all of my words come from solutions I have observed in my life and worldwide. In other words, I am not hypocritical so I will never speak on something I haven't actually dealt with firsthand and overcome.

If you are sensitive and not ready to face the truth about yourself, stop reading now and come back later when you can absorb things you have been ignoring or denying because whether you want to accept it or not, you have to follow core rules to go forward and maintain stability. Everybody wants a better life and so many people have the "answers", but in reality, the best path to take is the one designed especially for you. Everybody is different but these next several pages are your actual thoughts in front of your eyes written by someone that knows exactly how you feel. Yes, I am just like you, I had to face and overcome a lot of obstacles before realizing I was an asset to the world with my voice. I'm not going to stroke your back or kneel down and make you think magic is going to happen, I'm just going to show you the "regular" (no money or pre-existing joy needed) route to achieve wonderful things by simply breathing & learning from the moments you haven't been able to recognize. There are no fancy tricks or kits you need to buy, just a direct focus on reality while making it relevant in your spirit so that **YOU** can experience the true meaning of life.

I know this is rather new for you; I am in the same boat. I guess it would help if I addressed what I'm speaking of instead of jumping straight into our conversation. I am going to tie everything you have ever had questions about straight into a basic and universal understanding. It is a beautiful moment when you realize you're not alone in your struggles, all the questions that have been gripping your heart and making you the spiritual outcast starts to make sense for the duration of this journey called life.

We all live in the basic format, born into the world and attempting to develop an identity. We search for what makes us unique and different; the path that each person follows will vary on many levels based on experiences. None of us have the same story to tell, even if situations are similar. There is no standard pattern for each of our images with the drastic ups and downs of everyday living; no magazine article that documents the exact details of what makes the diversity will eventually show.

I awake each morning just to smile at myself in the mirror. Yes, that is my goal when I close my eyes at night; make it to see another moment of pure joy with waking up. The best feeling in the world is getting to know yourself and gain understanding for the balance you possess within. Only a struggle can bring victory because skating through not actually earning what you realize you deserve keeps you bound to ignorance that you will never be able to control. The first thing you have to do is realize you deserve it but we'll get to that with more reading. I reference these strong points because it is a part of sacrifice and humanity. There are some stories of individuals being born with "the silver spoon in their mouth" as coin phrased by Congress in 1801. I am not a history geek so don't think I am going to educate you, but I have to reach back and give credit where it is due. It started that long ago and passed right on through because anytime you hear it, you already know what it is. In short, it is someone who is born with an easy life and financial stability; they usually only lift a finger to point others in desired directions. Pretty nice life huh? Yeah, it probably is, but very few of those folks end up with a sense of reality and care for other human beings when they pursue their daily quest. Now you just read the words 'some' so I am not putting everyone in that category, please calm down and breathe, though I am sure I can find a panel of random minds to agree that it is quite a few folks floating around.

I really hope you are prepared to take this ride in 'straightforward gangsta' form because it is not cute. During this walk you might mess up your hair, your pants will definitely be wrinkled and please make an appointment to have those nails you are going to break fixed. We are going to fight in these pages, have a boxing match with your soul to defeat all the old views and swing into the elevated thinking you have been longing to approach. This isn't a book to judge you, remember I said I was just like you; this is just the Visine to clear your eyesight and see things like you have never been able to. I do not believe in giving anything 'coated in sugar', that would only hide the true taste of what you are going to swallow and it would disgrace my art of 'cooking' with real ingredients. This book will run your mind into a brick wall and put it right back together again without leaving a scratch. I must consider my mental stamina pretty powerful to go the long haul and be able to satisfy anyone reading this menu, huh? I do. I have lived a life that is only bringing more triumph with each flicker of hope that I provide to myself without anybody's help. Of course there are lessons I have learned through other people but it never connected in action until I gathered it all up and put it into full effect with my own concrete actions. Nothing in life is free, even for the people that can buy a city with the swipe of their credit card. There's still a price of spiritual value that must be paid eventually to go further with genuine success and purpose. I could care less about your position in life, the race has to be run and stripes must be given based on where you place the priority of honest results. This journey we are going to take together will boil the pot over with living in 'the now' and breaking free from the 'used to be'. I commend the population that was born knowing exactly what to do and how to do it and when to move and how far the diameter is to the center of your brain that controls the leaves blowing to the north of the artery instead of colliding with the lung to make decision making impossible. That sentence sounds ridiculous doesn't it? Well that's how you look to the rest of us that have overcome hurdles and wiped the sweat from our forehead because we chose to focus on doing things the right way. We would really like to offer you the opportunity to join this side and bask in a glow that would put the brightest light bulb to shame.

For those of you who have never encountered me before, I am very dramatic. I find it impossible (it's not really impossible, I just can't stand to be plain when expressing things) to just say, "Have a good day". What does that phrase mean? It deals with the same value across the board but it's so much more intriguing to say, "I hope the rise of your spirit will be cherished as the gift you received of new worth". Okay, okay, that is a bit much and not something you want to hear from your friend, but I like to throw the curve ball and bring it right up the center without flinching. I am not showing off, I just like to think "outside the box". I am not arrogant! How dare you say that, lol. I am really basic; I just paid close attention in Ms. Sneeden's 3rd grade class. She taught me so much, after I got glasses of course, and they stopped accusing me of just wanting to be disruptive but in reality I was blind as a bat. I gained my start with writing right there and did not even realize I would eventually go into this beautiful pool of displaying verbal art. That year I submitted an essay about whether radios should be allowed in school or was it a bad idea and I had to support my answers. Now any random eight or nine year old would LOVE to play music all day and jam out but I found the best description was going to come with NOT allowing the distraction. I can almost remember the elaboration but I am not that good. I did my chart of three main points and put three subs (A, B & C) underneath. Don't act like I am the only one that used that method, it was so effective. I might have been the class clown but I knew how to write.

I ran adults crazy, I moved how I wanted and kept the focus on me at all times. I will never be caught in a scandal because I will reveal my own past, flaws and all. Needless to say, I went through younger years as an outcast at school, home, the world, the air, life☐ yeah I'm doing it again, get used to the wonderful pictures I paint for understanding. Now you see why I KNOW I can relate to anybody? Right! I think bigger than what I think. It makes a lot of sense if you back it up to explain which is what I always do so nobody will be lost. Some of you got the little catch phrase I am drawing, and I am happy you are swift and ahead of the class, but life is not about being a brainiac, it is about the ability to apply. Nothing even matters if you just hold it and never know where or how to use it. 'I think bigger than what I think'....hmmmm, what does that mean? To me it means that just because I know something, I don't assume everyone gets things the same way. I have to step away from the norm and be big enough to accept folks for who they are and still have a clear understanding of what I'm trying to process without degrading my own mental capacity. Just because I have a large vocabulary doesn't mean I can't hold a meaningful conversation with someone that doesn't speak correct grammar;

there are so many ways to relate to another human being if you just "think bigger than what you think ". None of that means you are dumb or not as bright as I am because you don't use huge words to say hello, it just shows you have a different approach with the way you communicate. We live in a society that sets expectations for different people without being fair. I know in the past I have been guilty of saying things about folks because they do things a certain way or don't understand how to develop skills in their life and I learned that is definitely not the way to go. I had to learn over the years that my mind circulates differently than other people and that's perfectly normal. If we were all duplicates of another person, what in the world would we do about making different choices for individual needs? I don't like strawberries in syrup, the slimy feeling is gross, but I love strawberry milkshakes and strawberry flavored hard candy. Those are all the same flavors but depending on how it's presented, has a different appeal to me. That's the same with people; no matter how different people appear, we're all human once you remove the fancy bow.

I know without running into bad situations and without gaining assistance from different people, I would never be able to say I had any respect for life and all my moments lying on the ground. I haven't had to literally be on the ground, but I have had to get on my hands and knees in order to be given credit for hours worked, and a mop was my best friend. I have been to the lowest points of life before and I had no clue how I was going to make it because I always ignored the memo about growth and learning from my mistakes; I knew everything and nobody better even try to tell me I'm wrong. I was finally able to look at my own reflection and say 'I'm wrong'. I am so blessed that my instinct allowed me to bump my head once with different experiences and move forward, never dealing with the same misery twice. Oh but I bumped my head

quite a bit at various points of my life and skinned up my knees from tripping over my own feet, leaving me face down in the mud with humiliation. I used to be a wreck and it never seemed to change or get better, until I stopped moving so fast and I slowed down to evaluate reality.

As I mentioned in the beginning, the format of this whole book is not what most of you expect when reading. It's my unique presentation of things the way I see them and that's perfectly fine, the message will be delivered the way you NEED to receive it. Just like life, there's no official format, it just happens and makes sense when the time is right. There might be parts you read that have nothing to do with you but it might help your cousin or close friend. If my words make a difference for just one person, I am fulfilled and I have fully accomplished what I was aiming for. Nothing about me is normal so I'm not going to start a new trend just because this book will circulate around the world, I want to be received for who I am, not what I think others want. I'm sure everyone is familiar with social networking sites and the ability to write whatever is on your mind. When I post my thoughts, I tend to keep it very random yet brutally honest for the mass population to process. Basically, I write the first thing that comes to my mind and if it steps on your toes, move your feet or get new shoes, your choice. I always analyze things and find balance to relate with everyday folks or situations while expressing details of my personal experiences and what has worked in my life. I definitely express authentic thoughts on an open forum, no matter who likes it; I'm determined to never compromise my values or what I believe in. If you love my status updates or blog posts, you will adore this book; it is the expanded version of my mind, times 10. Enjoy.

*"No matter how wonderful you are, you can't make folks build a
relationship with you; there's a population of people that adore you just
because."*

A.D. Whittington

Eliminate negative energy completely.....

How many times has someone made you upset and you just can't seem to get over what they did? Or what about the devastating break-up that crushed your world? I am raising my hand for both those situations because I used to allow emotions to control my path. I would leave folks alone but they still had a huge effect on my life. The fact that my anger wouldn't fizzle and each time I would see him or her my blood would start simmering until I exploded from the boiling effect was exhausting and I kept missing the signs. Yes, we deleted each other off Facebook and there was absolutely no exchange through telephone communication, but I was glued in the corner of their control. I couldn't even move on and live in peace because I refused to let the moment die and live in my own wind. Staring at the thoughts everyday, talking junk when the name came up, hitting the wall with my fist and leaving a hole or very large dent because I'm that angry; all that energy to someone I would continually say didn't matter. Looks like they mattered a whole lot, enough to distract me from growing and taking care of my own mind. I couldn't move forward in any form or fashion, I had my spirit pinned to something that ultimately I had no control over. Sounds crazy now that you're seeing it spelled out in full, huh? It was the same revelation for me once I gained knowledge to free myself from the bondage. I get it, I'm definitely not talking smack because I'm better than you, just want to share the notes I have on what took place in my personal space.

I am the first to admit I used to be an emotional wreck when love entered the rooms of my heart. When I love, I love hard so I would always have a terrible battle with my inner balance when relationships would end. It's very simple yet so complex and it drags you to the ground. I mean, face in the dirt and blisters on the knees; the murdering of your mind and emotions is not a pretty picture. Trust me, I am way too familiar with the tears and runny nose because my insides would feel like they were crumbling into a million pieces. I used to find it hard to walk away from someone that I knew was not healthy for me, then I would allow myself to continue being abused by their actions or words; lying sick in bed because they couldn't, or better yet, refused to see my worth. Yes my dear, I know what you're feeling and the road still has to end. My whole world used to be on pause because I kept a grip with a vice claw, longing for answers I wanted to hear versus the moments of what was truly happening. Even though everyone on the outside could see it wasn't good for me, I always tried to justify to myself the reason I shouldn't give up. I had to literally dunk my head in a tank of cold-water [[[REALITY]]] to open my eyes. It hurt, it was frustrating, it took me to the bottom of the sea because I could never see that I was killing my life and it would never open into sunshine traveling the dangerous road of self-destruction.

When you say you want to walk away from negative friendships, relationships or people, you have to put forth so much effort to take responsibility and do what it takes for that fight. You can't just give in and keep dealing with it or standing in misery like the situation isn't painful to endure. You know it's bad, even if you don't admit it to others; nothing will change everything you suffer. No matter how much you hope & pray this will be the last time you are put out in the cold by the person that says 'I love you' daily, it's not. Have you taken time to know yourself and what you need in life? Stop settling for the minimum when your true value is much higher; your daily walk is not supposed to feel like rain with high winds that can destroy a city, you have to strive for sunny skies with comfortable temperatures.

"Just because others don't appreciate you doesn't mean you shouldn't have the utmost respect for yourself. You are your biggest fan, if the love doesn't exist in that arena, don't get upset w/ others for following your lead."

A.D. Whittington

"When you realize someone doesn't appreciate the wonderful person you know you are, no need in remaining stuck in that pain; confront your emotions & move forward."

A.D.Whittington

'The person you **KNOW** you are; but do you really **KNOW**? We all have experienced heartache and pain, whether it's with a romantic partner, close friend or family member; it stings and can break everything to pieces. Your life can be turned upside down in an instant with no view of how to get things back on track. I completely understand, I've gone through it too many times, hence the blueprint for writing this book. Everything I have ever felt or pushed past will be right here in front of your eyes and I'm not ashamed to admit I have dealt with less favorable circumstances at many different times of my life. It brought me to places that were very dark and left me wanting to hide in corners with no light. I would sometimes let other folks' actions control me so much, I couldn't put one foot in front of the other without seeking validation from outside forces. I know, that's horrible. I felt horrible but I had to face things directly to tackle the knots and kinks that stopped me from flowing in the right direction. I am all about having romance and friendship but after I discovered that nobody is responsible for my emotions besides me, I was able to release quite a bit and live in bliss. It's hard to change your life and do things out of your comfort zone but by the time we finish hanging out, I pray you will find peace and understanding with what makes you who you are.

It makes sense that you want the "relationship of your dreams" but if the other person doesn't give you the same, you need to expand your reach. Everybody is not meant to be connected in life and once you step into the realm of the heart mixed with the mind, controlling what you do can become very difficult. Start taking things slow, there's no rush to live, you will miss all the scenery.

How do you discover you are a wonderful person and truly believe it? Well, it starts with absolutely nothing. That's right, the mirror and you. No extra energy or money has to be spent, just focus on the vision you see and what the vision truly is; if the two don't match there's work to be done. Enlighten yourself about what makes you exist. Have you ever stopped to think about it? Honestly? You don't have to answer me or agree but it will not get better if you ignore or dodge the situation. This is a private ceremony you are involved in, no fancy clothes or image to uphold, just the raw core of your soul my dear.

You have to be able to admit you are struggling with things in your life, and then you can address the journey to find a solution. This is just the surface of how deep this thing goes, it can never be scratched if you don't at least try to locate the itch.

Now you like to say you're confident and centered with life but the first person looking at you wrong sends you into a downward spiral. Doesn't seem too stable to me, looks like you need restructure at the foundation. You will meet thousands of people in the world and there is no way you will vibe for a bond with all of them. Not because any of you are bad people but because you're all different. According to Webster's Dictionary the definition of one of the most important words for your vocabulary speaks for itself; *in·di·vid·u·al·i·ty-: separate or distinct existence.* You have to stand out from the crowd and confirm your confidence within, never straying from the path you set. It's called having a backbone for yourself, good old fashion sticking up your dukes and fighting for the most important person you ever met. It's a requirement and never needs to be placed in another slot besides first with your thinking. I am definitely not going to pacify you but I am going to help you through this land you're lost in if **YOU** want to be found. Nobody can make you want this; it's not a trending topic on any network so remove superficial thoughts and prepare for authentic excellence my friend.

This is something only you can process, don't worry about anyone else, it's your journey. I already know you want to reach out to people you're used to connecting with because it gets hard to break the routine, but the things you have been doing aren't working so time to try something new; evolution of your life the right way. Nothing like grabbing the profound emotions you are fighting in your spirit and making them your new habits. You might not understand but when this is over you will definitely agree. It's cool to be grounded, you won't be changing everything today and things will adjust according to what is required for **YOUR** life. This whole experience is for somebody that has been crying and begging for relief but they have no clue how to get it or even where to start. It's common to worry about what other people might say or think but there comes a time when you have to become selfish for your own sake of survival in life. I get it, I was there and I am rooting for you. If you feel alone with those you know, just trust the fact that there are folks that understand and they are just waiting on you to join their circle of unconditional and true love.

This page was left blank intentionally; the best form of therapy is self-expression. You might not be a writer but your thoughts don't need a format.

"Someone being 'emotional' doesn't mean they are 'crazy' or 'irrational', it just means they are human."

A.D.Whittington

People are all different so before you talk junk about someone because they shed tears or react in a big way, think about the fact that they are human. I'm not saying it's okay for people to run around and do things that hurt others, but before you pass judgment, put yourself in their shoes. Would you yell if your feelings were hurt or would you be calm and let it slide? Yeah, you never know why your friend's ex was chasing you all at top speeds and throwing bottles at the car when you pulled out of the parking lot. Did your friend tell you that they were leading the ex on then ignored all calls before being caught with another romantic interest? Come on, you know you would flip out and cause a huge scene, why are you telling everyone that you just encountered a psychotic person? You know how your friend is; don't forget there's more to the story and if you think hard enough, you can figure out the missing parts.

THE BRAND:

Where did these little stick people come from? I am amazed at how they were given life and just how much they mean to this book. Jamal Williams is a genius with creating things through graphic design and he didn't fail with this project. We were sitting in the living room of my home with Lola Brooks trying to create a cover that would represent the contents of the book on sight. Lola started throwing out ideas about stick figures and inviting colors and as she was becoming more animated, Jamal was clicking his mouse to develop my new brand, the images with no face. After we analyzed their positions on the screen we were able to give them their role. The first image is pointing the blame to the far right. The image to the far right is not taking any of this serious and just dancing through without a care but the one in the middle is victorious by accepting responsibility and feeling great about the victory. That was so simple yet so universal for what we see everyday. Now we needed a colorful background that would grab everyone's attention but not scare folks away; the first perception would either intrigue or distract readers. After several colors were attempted, the warm spring green won, hands down. I then told Jamal exactly how I wanted the letters to sit and shadow; he had it pulled together in a matter of seconds. We continued analyzing every approach to make sure this was the final design and after moving all the images and lettering a few inches left or right, the face of responsibility was created for the profound words you all are getting the opportunity to read. I hope this book is truly helping people see the reality of their life based on their actions.

"I don't conform to what others WANT me to be or represent, I want my unique existence to have meant something concrete when I leave this earth."

A.D.Whittington

Expired Bandwagons

Hello sunshine, I am so glad you're still reading. I have a lot on my mind so prepare to be enlightened. The main focus circulating in my mental right now are all my own thoughts, which brings me to a very important topic; thinking for yourself. "No A.D., say it ain't so". Yes my friend, it's a plague these days.

The fact that anyone has a life designed by others because they do not live for self is troubling, but it must be given the proper voice. I have such a strong personality and mind, there's not much I believe or just "go with" without thorough research. Never have I gone into a situation blind without full evaluation of all the energy surrounding the scene. When I interact with others, I never pass judgment based on the general opinion of the "public"; I stop and watch intensely for my own connection or lack of.

There are going to be people you encounter that absolutely nobody likes, but it is not fair to him or her for **YOU** to automatically jump in the car with all these other drivers and not take the road test yourself. The factors that are causing bad vibes could stem from things you aren't aware of. Who knows what occurred to get individuals separated at the seam and rustled beyond repair? The diversity of the world
brings different levels of souls mixing at weird

times and the degree of difficulty could be extremely unique, causing a ripple in the natural order.

Stop being a follower of everything you hear, you don't know what's really going on, and you decided it was right just because you like the person talking. Half of what is being discussed may be false and not hold a lick of merit; you have to survey the source of the knowledge. Are they even reliable with the reality of life? What really transpired between the folks you're discussing? Was it random but now being pounced on from a place of hurt and anger developed by a scarred soul?

I definitely stick to my own words of advice. There can be 100 people in the room that hate a particular group or person, but until I see negative energy for myself, I have to stay in my lane and be okay with the scene. There could very easily be a story of dislike because particular individuals don't follow the way of the "norm" or they don't practice being just like everyone "thinks" they should, but no truly valid reasons for the disconnection from everyone else. Where is the book that says behavior has to be patterned a certain way to matter? Who is the deciding point on separate thinking and what is precisely "right" or "wrong"? I mean, let's be real, how do you know the truth without personal validation?

Don't get me wrong, all accusations might be right, but how in the world can you stamp that with your mind and live unconditionally with your choice? How can you possibly have tarnished friendships and relationships before giving it a chance, just because there's a circulation of the "wrong" influence? People are intimidated by direct and honest presence, so that alone will build a wall that is unjust and bias. I get so annoyed by the population of non-thinkers, showing that they have the backbone of a wet noodle and a brain that is sitting on a pile of quicksand.

I have made it a point to surround myself with the necessary balance so I don't get caught up in a whirlwind of "gossip" or meaningless focus. I can take what is being given as a gift when it goes the right direction but I never get trapped in the wreckage of overwhelming rubbish. I am so blessed that my life holds concrete foundation and when the planets orbit in my mind, it never knocks me into the universe of absent living. I am proud that I always give a fair shake to available opportunities and I feel the growth of wonderful connections based on what I have avoided; never being caught on a broken carousel that keeps going around with a collapsed handle and showing no signs of stopping or changing directions, just helpless thoughts in the never-ending sky.

RANDOM:

That is my middle name; I am all over the place sometimes, lol. I don't have an official format for this thing called life, I just make things go with the flow of what works best.

I don't love sweets but I do get an urge for certain things on occasion. Lemon cake with a light glaze is one of my favorites; I appreciate Sheila Rogers making that and saving me a slice so I could lose my mind with the fork, lol. I would like some pumpkin strudel but I guess I'll have to wait until the holidays when she decides to bless my stomach once more.

Smarties is my absolute favorite candy, I eat at least 5 bags a week. Don't judge me, they keep me going.

Bath and Body Works has the best scents for the spring and summer but I can definitely do without their winter choices. If they could just keep Island Margarita for 12 months, I would be content.

"Just because someone pursues different goals than you doesn't mean their venture isn't valid; individuality is a word everyone should know."

A.D. Whittington

Always think for yourself and don't worry about others....

It really isn't important what others think about you; all that matters is what you feel in your heart about yourself. I know we all want those around to love us and care about our well being, but the reality is, it won't always happen that way. That should never stop you from striving to do the best job at being you; it is the only job you were truly created for. So what you have some goofy traits, they are you, and if someone is intended to be in your personal space, they will love it. You will definitely have to cut a lot of things and people loose once you start in the direction of change; it's just a factor in this equation. You need to sit down and look at what stands strong versus what stands in the way. I know you're going to have a hard time changing a few things but it gets easier the more you connect with a better flow of positive energy.

You don't need to make excuses for that friend you have had for many years, even though that friend has slept with a love interest knowing the circumstances of your heart attached to that person. What makes that okay, ever? I'm not telling you to start a fire and burn down their house or jump on Facebook and update statuses about the situation, but you need to update the status of your soul and get away from that "friendship". One thing I have realized is that the "wrong" people will leave you completely alone when you change for the better. It doesn't make sense but it's the truth, plain & simple. When you're caught up in everybody's drama and running the streets with no purpose, folks love you to death. They love the fact you struggle with friendships and can't hold a job; it makes them happy to see you are getting high every night & not maintaining purpose. It sounds stupid but it's the way the vibe seems to go in life.

I'm not pinning that on everybody so don't take offense unless it applies, but those that aren't in a place of positive elevation will definitely fall away and turn away from all your attempts to progress. That's how you will know; the environment changes and you start to notice "people don't like you anymore", for no apparent reason. To you it seems sudden, and it is, but it is for a valid reason. The reason they start talking about you all the time or stabbing you in the back every chance they get is because they're mad they aren't headed in the same direction as you. They can say all day they have started to grow and become more mature but if it's not genuine, you will always be moving way too fast and they can't possibly keep up. It's not in them so there's no need to try and make them. When it's their time to be in a better place, it will happen, until then it will only frustrate you and make you feel lost when it comes to having a relationship with your "best friend".

I used to get upset or have hurt feelings when I would try and help someone but they wouldn't just jump on the train and change their life. It used to sting my heart and make me cry when people would receive my help, even though secretly they didn't appreciate it, and run to the streets and slay my name and my character. I could never understand how someone I let stay in my home because they had nowhere to go could even allow my name to cross their lips with bad things to tell others. How can you hurt a person that has shown you nothing but support when every choice you made before that point was ignorant? I racked my brain but the answer stayed hidden, until I learned more about people. I see that it is the nature of some individuals to go with what works instead of standing up for what's right. It just works better for their simple brains to get in little groups and discuss me as a topic, trying to find the negative things that will tear me down. The group meetings are always a compliment because I am so powerful as a person spiritually and mentally, it takes more than one person to collect things and try to search for whatever can make me out to be the bad guy. If I was so horrible, a group meeting or conference call wouldn't be necessary, one person having the information would be strong enough to defeat my efforts & the signs would show to everyone else in EVERY area of my life.

I am on a mission to help others but I can't let others tear me down. When folks complain about me, I can't just go with what they say; they're too lost for me to trust. How in the world is there a huge population of people that know me well and will give me the straight edge of the razor if I'm wrong (trust me, it happens from my true friends, that's how I know they're true friends, duhhh) but someone that is caught up in their own maze with no sight of the end wants to point out things I should change??? I can't trust your opinions about me, the ones you have for yourself suck so I am sure you don't have the first clue of what real love and a good person is. I realized I am always a problem for someone that doesn't have his or her "stuff" together. Next time you hear someone taking mess about another person, look at the source of the information. Are they educated, stable, happy with who they are, striving for better, lost in love, independent, fragile, always trying to fit in even though some people think they're popular (they just blend in really well, even though they're not being who they are but it's a great act), jealous of that person's success, mad about that person's ability to be who they are, upset they don't have the balls to do what they're whining about, etc., etc., etc.??? That was a quite a bit but that's just how sad the situation will become when there's no true grounds for all that negative energy floating around. Once these weak and lost people state their case, they search for others just like them to validate feelings that still mean nothing. HA! Still losing but even more dangerous because you add extra poison to the potion.

I don't expect some of you to understand, not asking you to, just giving you details based on my growth through painful lessons learned. I will never try and be what another wants because I am in control of learning what truly works for me in time. Everyone's speed is very different on his or her separate path; what works for one more than likely will not work for another at the same time. The process takes flight when the runway to someone's life is clear for the landing. Don't set your tone based on those around you, get to know your inner soul so that you can speak up when necessary and you won't be held hostage by the prisons of yours or other people's shattered minds. The defense team will be a lot stronger when you can stand up for yourself with personal facts developed in your life instead of stealing notes from somebody else.

"I don't want to do what makes other folks happy, I just want to do what's right."

It's My Fault....

"Don't be mad because I'm who I am & I embrace that; take it up w/ the Man upstairs, He did it. Focus on being your best you, God has enough to go around."

A.D.WHITTINGTON

Beautiful Gifts

Take a moment to be excited like you just won the lottery or you placed a bid on a new house and your realtor called to tell you that your offer was received. Be overjoyed that you are able to read these words and navigate through different areas of information; your mind is steady and constantly growing. I am grateful for inspiration and views of broad spectrums, without those simple areas I would be cast into an area of dark ignorance that has no sign of light. Make sure you do not take anything for granted, the hidden blessings included, it could be so much worse.

A lot of times we push precious moments to a place of little value and we don't look at what the standard could really be for our existence. Someone may be homeless or a drug addict but he or she is still a person. You are not above the point to reflect and see how that could have been you. Your mind happens to be stronger and on a different path, but the blood is still red, running warm through your veins. A major thanks goes out to the ability of direction for self, allowing the choices of success to be stronger in our hearts.

They are probably sad they went down that path but we all make mistakes we want to retract. I didn't say give them your car or let them hold your wallet while you use the restroom, I am just putting emphasis on respect for the things we don't give meaning in our personal space. It's easy to be grateful for the material things or great job, why wouldn't you? I definitely feel those are major, just include everything when recognizing your worth. I'm sorry to tell you but you're not better than anyone, you just happen to have a focus that's grown in a different direction. Be fully aware of what people mean to the world and don't forget about the deeper things that keep the clocks turning in the simplest fashion.

"True friendship is just as precious as an intimate relationship, they should both be cherished & held in top priority."

"A true friend never makes you feel uncomfortable about being who you are or standing strong by the decisions you make....I truly appreciate the folks God has blessed me with who understand me as a person and respect things I do in my life that are designed to work for me."

A.D.Whittington

Solid Foundations

I am not gonna (gonna: regular talk for getting ready to do something) keep you long because what I have on my heart doesn't require a lot of rambling or extra conversation. I want everybody to sit down and evaluate actual emotions for others. What do you carry for those you consider to be your friend? How about one step further, the ultimate position to assign to another human being ➜➜➜★THE BEST FRIEND???

I guess I get confused because so many folks jump on that road and have no clue about the terms. I meet people and the day we communicate, they call me their best friend. How do you know I will be the BEST you will ever have in life? Stop claiming me all over the internet and telling everyone I'm your sister but you can't tell me what size shoe I wear or my favorite food. This thing has to go both ways and I don't agree with taking the job because I ain't (yes I said ain't) gonna put you down as a contact on any form of paperwork, I don't take it light at all. Granted I'm a wonderful person, full of honesty and love; no fake feelings in sight, but how do you know that? You spoke with me and love my energy, but I am not your best friend, I'm just naturally a good person that you can be honest with but I have my doubts about you so I don't think this is going to work for us as a team.

I think being a friend is key but the role of BEST FRIEND is superb amongst anyone you associate with, it should be the ultimate level of being true.

I listen to people refer to their "best friend" but in the next sentence say they don't trust them or they're scared to reveal something to them for fear of what they will think. What do you mean they aren't always there for you and you know they're talking about you behind your back? That's the BEST you can do in life? Nobody else was available to take that spot? Wow! I would say you should evaluate everything you ever thought to be genuine in your mind, about yourself.

Number one thing that annoys me, besides undercooked meat, is when folks throw that term around~~~>BEST FRIEND!!! I DO NOT believe that all "best friends" fulfill the duty of following through in the most sincere fashion. When folks introduce someone as their BEST FRIEND, I automatically start scanning their interaction to see if they truly give that title a valid home in the heart. Just because you have known someone forever doesn't make them your best friend, it means you have known another person for a long time; simple!!! How could you consider someone who sleeps with your mate, lies to you, tells secrets that are common, continues to shed no light on your growth, uses you, refuses to be stable with their loyalty, and on and on and on and on and on I can go, an important bracket to what you want in companionship? If I can't be myself and share my deepest passions without saying, "Don't tell anybody" because your mouth runs on a diesel engine, you are far from getting close to the role of BEST FRIEND in my personal space.

I value people I love and truly need to be connected with spiritual substance on a regular basis. To be a BEST FRIEND in any form to me it takes more than lunch together on occasion or a fashionable style of dress, it has to be a natural bond that GROWS to be strong and full of unthinkable wonder. I can't say I keep many folks around because if you're not of good nature and intent to my loved ones and myself, the interview stops immediately, and you are no longer in the running for becoming 'America's Next Top Friend'.

"In life, communication is the key to all things growing to a better place. We must practice being honest and allowing our feelings to be direct with the people and situations most involved. Hiding behind the computer screen or other barriers that will not resolve life only leads to more sorrow; be open to confronting things for solid and positive resolution."

A.D. Whittington

Communication is key....

At one point in my life, I was far from perfect and I'm still a work in progress. I have traveled to this land of maturity where I learned from all my mistakes; do not think for one second you have to stay frozen in time for failure. It takes a strong person to admit areas of weakness and address the solutions with an open mind. We all face difficult choices to become better and build healthy defenses against our negative past. Stop whining and expecting an award, it is what it is. Regardless to what you want to happen, the truth of all things is that you will never advance if you can't communicate effectively.

I didn't say you're a loser because you can't speak in big words or make these profound statements when attempting to connect with the outside world. Did you just misunderstand what I typed and jump into resistance because you could really care less, even though you have no friendships worthy of reporting and your last 3 mates had to bail due to your lack of communicating? There were two of you with a voice, but you always refused to hear the other side when it didn't follow your script of words when you talked to your "boo". I agree, you should definitely go the other way because what you're doing is perfect genius.

I get so tired of hearing excuses for the 'lack-of-communication' trait. What in the world people? If you are the victim of this emotional wrecking ball, you might want to give a copy of what you're reading to the person guilty of the action I speak of, I don't know them but they can benefit from all this advice. I refuse to hold my own thought silent, that's why I wrote this book; I wanted to express genuine thoughts that people worldwide might find useful. I live an expressive life with lots of communicating because without it, all that empty space can gather questions and confusion that could very easily be avoided if words were exchanged.

The only bridge to connect facts that float around inside is by telling others. No, you don't have to walk up to random strangers and start spilling all your business, but you do have to communicate polite gestures simply because they are a human being. Stop over-analyzing, you don't have to kiss their hand, but come on, is it horrible to hold the darn door or say 'excuse me'? Geesh, this isn't rocket science, just courtesy man. I have to grab my inner-thug and let it roll in straight terms, no ketchup to dress it up, just hot sauce on the shake (I think I'm witty sometimes, might not be true but I go with it).

And these relationships in 2012 are hurting! There is no way you guys are happy with each other but you do not communicate effectively. I have yet to find stability in a union that is based on sign language or assumptions. Why is someone you "love" subjected to your absent affection? You never spoke a word about what you want but now you're upset because the other person didn't read your mind and just jump off the bridge as you have instructed mentally. And let's stop the train all together because you always want to say what you feel but hold tape over his or her mouth so they can't respond. What kind of mess is that? Oh, I forgot, you really need to date yourself so your objective is all that counts, but you're too selfish to let your "love" go; holding it hostage for personal gratification. You are tripping, HARD!! I don't know how to pretty that one up. I used to be one-tracked with my mates but I had to finally see the road I was paving with dusty gravel and spikes; tearing up the tires of their heart and never slowing down to offer assistance. I was in that zone years ago; I definitely could not talk about this if I had not experienced the survival. I had to feel complete remorse for my egotistical habits and present more positive reinforcement with my behavior.

You have not even communicated with your friend to see what they meant with their gestures the other day, instead you just hold it in and walk around mad because it LOOKED like they were trying to ignore you and talk about you behind your back. Did it ever dawn on you they might be going through a tragedy they do not want to share with you? They're human, but since your blinders are on to only your inner sorrow, you don't check and see the true problem. And what about the "new girl", that some people have said is trouble? Hmmmm, maybe since you came at her the wrong way she has her defenses up but she is actually super sweet; yet again, you're lost in the rafters because you would much rather hold hostility against rumors and not just walk over and see what her personality is really like for yourself.

This is a lot to read but I could not cut any corners, the truth is heavy on my heart. I live in the same society you're in and I am flat out tired. Am I going to change everything right now? Heck no, not expecting that, just want at least one person to do a silent evaluation for a complete revelation in his or her private space. Be fair to each other; give what you would like to receive. You don't want to be yelled at for someone to communicate his or her thoughts, DON'T DO IT TO OTHERS. I don't care that you're hard; you still feel pain when certain things are said, or not said at all. Stop forming opinions to hold as the final theory towards groups or individuals you have not been gracious enough to extend direct contact with, forming your own assessment after what boys and girls?? COMMUNICATE and get involved. Be unique and break away from the crowd, it feels clean on your spirit my friend. Communication is vital on a daily basis, don't fall off thinking you are right because you're not, and I hope you will practice your new way right after you finish this sentence.

You ever notice that when you're in a rush to get somewhere, every light in town turns red just as you're approaching, deflating any hope of making through to the next corner? When I leave home in enough time, I have the easiest travel time and end up early.

When it's raining I can never find a parking spot close to the building I'm going in.

I'm addicted to clearance racks and great sales; the quality is still the same, just at an affordable price, which means I can get more. YEHHHHHH!!!!!

I don't have a favorite color, I like items based on what they look like in a particular shade.

I do not like horror movies or Amusement Park rides; I just can't see the logic in paying to scare myself silly.

I love to play games at Chuck E. Cheese. I'm not sure how I'm going to age; I still have very immature hobbies, lol.

"You don't have to force what's meant to fit naturally; it will just flow in a smooth fashion without a struggle."

It's My Fault....

"Be careful who you confide in, not everyone will protect your thoughts and feelings with love & respect."

A.D. Whittington

You can't please everyone....

I say this all the time but it will remain a solid part of my daily conversation; I am not a doctor but I have a degree with life experiences as the internship. I strive to do the right thing and when I don't, I evaluate my flaws and adjust to become a better me. I urge you to do the same thing because you are truly blessed to touch the ground each morning and take in deep breaths so your lungs can filter the garbage in the air. Well pollution isn't a treat, but you get my point.

I want to extend my hand to someone that is fighting with his or her own internal weakness right now. I know that the road you have been traveling seems to be taking a turn into a dark tunnel but it is just preparation for good things ahead. I know, I know, it is killing your spirit and you want to give up, but it gets better.

All the people that are in your personal space and generating negative vibes have a hold on your spirit and you have to cut that off. It's not easy but you have to make the attempt so that the actual mission of growing can become and stay solid. It isn't easy being you and not many people will understand your motives so I'm not just giving you a solution that makes no sense because I don't understand exactly how you feel. I know too well how you feel and I remember the struggle I had when I changed my environment and people around me. I was a talked about and called a name or two, but I knew my life would never be fixed if I didn't initiate it with determination. It is a task to build friendships because thoughts of betrayal aren't far behind. You probably cry quite a bit because those you lean on keep moving and showing no embrace. I get it, I lived it. I didn't know then but it was a blessing to be treated in a bad way and have my soul spit on with harsh words because it forced me to lean on me.

I am not trying to pacify you, that's not possible to do when it all comes to light, I am simply showing you the slight vision you are having a hard time finding. You keep fumbling on the wall to flip the switch on but check your pocket; it's in plain sight. Nothing in life is easy and you definitely can't set your sights on others for the solution to your problems. I am not saying you will never need outside forces to assist but that's all it should be, tools to lend a hand, not the sole means of survival.

People are going to talk about you; stop letting their attacks bring you down. None of the madness will cease to exist or slow down and the more emotion you invest, the easier you make it for folks that have no true life of their own to find distraction with your pain. They don't have to look far for misery, they have it right in front of their face, watching you crumble and without realizing it, you always give them a fresh show. I practice doing the right thing in life but people still have an issue when I don't jump at the very second they want me to. My life isn't about pleasing other people because if I'm not happy and secure with finances, emotions and spiritual wealth, I'm not much good to anybody. I find that I upset people constantly and they say I let them down but there's no way for me to control every little thing that happens when it comes to others.

I didn't attend someone's function and it was communicated that I disappointed that person. It made me stop to think about the things being said, but once I evaluated the complete scenario, I had to step back and feel good about my presence in life. Yes, it would be great if I could be in fifty places at once but not one word was uttered to see WHY I didn't make it. The fact that I reached out to connect with concern about missing the function wasn't important either; it just matters that I didn't go, even though I go to all other events and show support. I'm not trying to vent, there's nothing to vent about, but it's an example of how I roll forward after going through the checklist in my brain and accept the positive things about myself. If I am such a friend that gives unconditional love at all times, why wasn't this person that same type of friend to care about my personal issues and check on me? I get the whole 'hurt-when-you-feel-alone' emotion, but have you factored in all details to analyze the core of the person you're passing these unrealistic judgments on? I can't be put into this pool of 'people that don't care' just because I hurt someone's feelings by not showing up, but the things I was dealing with in my personal space are far more important to my well being and personal sacrifice; I have to care about those things first. Of course my "friend" didn't get that specific memo because selfish thinking was driving their ship into the dock when it crashed. Yes that thought ran on and on and on, and won't be corrected when proof reading because it was intentional, just like the moments of silence when I had to look at reality and what I allow to have an affect on my journey. I analyze everything in the world and one thing I do know about most human beings is that they give the person that shows they care the hardest time, because that person DOES show they care, but others that don't show unconditional love get the most energy invested into a "friendship of nothing". I will never get that and I gave up trying, I just stay on the path to holding my head high and allow people that accept and respect my existence open invitations into my intimate level of love; my heart.

When I can take a deep look at things I endure and the answer gives me peace because I know my stance in life, nobody can bring me down or make me feel worthless. You are supposed to love your family and friends but you have to love yourself first. If me not attending an event will determine the value you place on our connection as friends, it was shallow to begin with and doesn't have a future worth mentioning. Make the things you stress over worth an emotion, you are the one that will be suffering for a long time and others will be going forward; not giving you a second thought. Have more understanding for what you mean to life, you're not perfect. If you're doing the best you can with what you have, the rest is irrelevant because you won't always be able to get folks to jump for joy with each victory you claim. I pray you can find a deeper push to lift yourself over the brick wall you built and take off running through the field of lilies in your mind.

"It's amazing how some folks put expectations on others that they don't even practice themselves."

This one is pretty simple and you might be reading it as though it's out of place. It really is but there are so many people that are truly living in their own world and assume others are wrong for things they do. I watch folks get upset because someone doesn't do something they like or want and I just give them the blank stare because I know they don't practice what they are demanding. There is no way you can be mad with your friends for not inviting you out with them but you do your own thing without inviting them all the time. Really?? You're serious about it too but I am here to tell you that you're wrong. You're not a special icon that folks should run around spreading roses on the ground for; you're a regular person just like everybody else.

Spiritual Decorum

My bright and colorful vibes are blessing you with a ((((HUG)))) as you join in the whirlwind of joy located in the high areas of your day; it is such a pleasure to give true balance to souls of appreciation.

I am giving simple thoughts to open minds. No fancy doodles or whistles blowing as I open the door of mental growth for all to pass through. I have some strong words for you to chew and swallow that won't cause decay; quite simply put, there is no cost in being courteous to other human beings. I do not use extra energy when I give a smile, or modestly wave with great vibrations. I find joy when I hold the door for an approaching stranger; it makes me feel complete in the department of gracious giving. The warmest feelings are taken from my heart with satisfaction because I know every effort is concrete and thorough with no leaks of insecurity pushing me into the ocean of negative results.

I challenge you to be unnecessarily pleasant toward another human being or be simple and sweet when saying thank you to the cashier taking time to double bag your groceries. Wave at the guy who has a physical deformity and speak to the lady mopping the floor at the store you frequent each week; never realizing she looks tired because she works two jobs aside from nurturing a family in this society we forget can kill anyone's spirit. I am asking you to venture into areas of love that are critical but won't eliminate important stamina in life or cause danger to you physically; I ask you to join me and display behavior we all can be proud of in making a difference for all that truly matter; innocent souls that bear the joys of life.

"I don't get upset that people don't feel the same about me as I do them, I just hate how long it takes me to realize it sometimes #realitycheck"

It's My Fault....

"You can only do so much to try & make folks happy; when your BEST isn't good enough, it's ok to let go so you can maintain a healthy life for yourself. You're all you've got, don't ever allow anyone to destroy that priceless foundation."

A.D.Whittington

You don't need approval to drive forward....

One of the biggest struggles for a lot of people is that they want to be accepted just the way they are. I have to admit, I had an extremely difficult time with that journey myself so I'm sharing the same hurt emotions many of you carry or those you know have experienced. I had to learn to disregard others and live by my own opinions and thoughts. Nobody can determine exactly what works for you, they haven't been in your shoes and have no clue why you operate in the manner you do.

I'm just hitting on a couple things that came across my spirit so this is all straight from my heart. Of course that's how I always express, with honest words to enlighten, but recently I had to face one of my biggest fears, reality. I have been connected with lots of people and not everything goes in the direction I desire. There are relationships I used to long for with family members and lost friends, but after dealing with my own weaknesses, I came out of the storm refreshed and ready to drive at full speed.

I'm not going to bash anyone on this post, no need to be harsh, because at the end of the day, I evolved victorious; I have already conquered that demon. I know I used to allow my emotions to take over my logic and I would become consumed with everything anyone said against me. I would let their lack of open understanding distract me from being productive towards MY growth. There's nothing wrong with realizing that people not understanding you can be a measure of their love, but it's not all right to fall completely in the lake and drown in sorrow. I can't whimper in the corner and cry for days trying to figure out WHYYYYYY???? That question might not ever be answered so I had to gather my dignity and drive through the barriers to grab the gold medal.

Do I get upset when someone that says they love me speaks negative about me? To be honest, sometimes I get fighting mad. Do I stay planted in that moment for more than 2 minutes? NOPE! I have discovered that I can't deal with the rough spots that lead nowhere so I throw them out the window. No matter what your "title" is in my personal space, once I see you're unhealthy, I truly move past you. Not because I'm upset or hurt, I have to go forward because I grasp the concept you are who you are and it's not good for my journey. Some people like to think that what they do causes me to spiral down but the truth is simple, you don't deserve any emotion so no need in flattering yourself as being that important because you're not. You are a human being but not someone I find gratitude in showing my attention to. Regardless to what others say, if you don't hear the details from me directly, you might want to deflate your big head of air and wait on the brutally honest feedback I will most certainly supply to you for myself.

I know you want your family to accept your homosexual lifestyle but you're a loving human being that strives to do the right thing; don't let the rejection beat you in the chest and stop your breathing. I know it stings that your parents want you to marry that guy with money but if your heart is attached to the guy that is searching for a better business to provide for his family, you can't let your true love walk out the door and neglect your own spiritual stability. Your children are mixed with another culture but the only crime with that is listening to ignorant people pass judgment and attempt to draw you out of the bright focus you have on your future so they can be settled in their insecurities. I know I wrote about NOT allowing others to control your emotions and this might be a repeat but you can never address the topic enough, the chains must be broken so the cycle can be stopped and driven into the ashes of that miserable fire called FAILURE. You don't need to walk around feeling any obligation to others; you have to tackle that action with yourself first because without the first wall being constructed with proper pressure, the entire structure will eventually crumble.

You've read quite a bit by now; there are definitely some important thoughts you can write in this section. It doesn't have to be bad or even about yourself but what difference is this book making in your personal space?

"I have about 2 million units of positive energy to share. It comes w/ a complimentary supply of peace & balance, no charge. Anyone interested please grab what you need; feel free to pass along to others ***in the narrator's voice talking super fast====[advertisement paid for by A.D. Whittington's campaign to strive for better, sponsored by her daily blessings]."

A.D.Whittington

Momentary Forever

Sending beautiful rays as you journey, even if you're reading this in the middle of the night, the energy last for eternity. The joy of this awakening is you have the chance to give fresh meaning to anything that needs adjusting. If things were not complete and in order before you slumbered hours ago, here's a chance to be a better you.

Make sure you are giving energy to thoughts and actions that are productive. Why consume your personal space with meaningless actions, stimulating unnecessary things to be set in motion? What exactly is going to come from you being in a frenzy toward a situation that will still have the same outcome, whether you're stressed about it or not?

In life, things are lined up with the universe and if it's destined to happen, you will see the finished product in your lap. If the lines don't coordinate with each other, no matter how upset you are, you will then just have devastated emotions to sort out and still stand with the cracked egg in your palms looking for a paper towel but remain aggravated that it's still slipping through your fingers.

I always had many wishes on getting further in life but if it wasn't my time; I had to come to peace in my heart with mature understanding.

Sometimes we aren't supposed to be where we WANT to be, we have to accept being we are supposed to be for our particular energy level.

Next time you apply for a job and don't get it, even though you KNOW you're the best candidate, don't get upset or feel like a failure; just know deep inside your inner spirit it wasn't for you. No need in being disappointed for too long when it has nothing to do with you, it was all in the timing. When going high and free, you might be rejected momentarily but appreciate the extra time for possible improvements and preparation once the time IS right in your life. I don't know about you, but I never put new clothes on the basket of dirty laundry, I clean everything and when it is time, I put everything in it's respective places. Work on revising yourself so that when your blessings arrive, you will have the 'minor-things-that-have-the-capability-of-escalating-to-frustration-when - you're-overwhelmed' all sorted out for much easier living standards.

"So, you're mad w/ the world because you made poor choices even though other options you refuse to try are available? Makes sense! (NOT REALLY)"

It's My Fault....

"Stop expecting different results but your actions never change. You sir/ma'am are not special, everybody has to process reality."

A.D.Whittington

Breakfast Bar

I am here in a great spirit and I want to share some of my "food" so you can run on full speed for the obstacles that might come your way. Take a bite of this focus so that negative distractions won't throw you completely into the fire of being lost. A lot of times we get side tracked on things that will not assist with completing task & priorities we are destined to accomplish for success; give your attention to the greater cause of self, there's nothing more important. I think a bowl of spiritual balance will stick to the ribs and keep you feeling whole, nothing like running the mile in record time because stability was concrete to keep you pushing forward.

I really hope you enjoy the side of strength with the spread of love; it's absolutely delicious when served together. When your heart is pure and all intentions point to yes, you have to know in your soul that things will always be just fine. I know it gets discouraging to try your best and feel there is no true appreciation for your existence, but keep things wrapped close in your heart so nothing can allow doubt to overwhelm your space of solid well-being. I have some more items on this open bar of scrumptious substance, take your time to taste and decide what will fit your appetite of growth.

"I'm far from perfect but the fact I have desires to strive for better each day is all the perfection required for spiritual balance. Everyone is different, our journey & lessons learned will vary but it doesn't mean we don't have the same passion for life. You don't have to like me but you have to respect honesty, for your own good."

A.D. Whittington

The Mere Thought....

I believe in life that all things have only two solutions; in your favor or against. At the point you realize what a situation is based on, you should focus on resolving it with no extra clouds being permitted in your mental space. It is so important to stay at a calm peace in your mind and not go off into another mental wreck because it is very difficult to return back to sanity. I realize life has stress and sometimes your emotional buttons can be pushed to the point they almost pop off. I also know that stress is a part of daily functions and will never be completely avoided, but we can control how we conduct ourselves in response to any issue.

I always like to use the example of losing your keys. That is one of the common things that happens to most of us isn't it? You NEED your keys to drive your vehicle and if you lose them, HOW AM I GONNA GET TO WORK, I'M GONNA LOSE MY JOB?!?!?!? That's where most of you go in your mind when you have looked everywhere and still no keys. Most individuals possess the minimum amount of keys but those few are so important for opening doors, literally, and proceeding with your day.

Very important you say? I do agree. Definitely a valid reason to panic out of control when they are lost but it's still not going to find the keys. Okay A.D., you're contradicting yourself. Of course I am, to you; how else will you find the keys unless you run around yelling at anyone in the vicinity and breaking into a huge sweat? (Maybe that's a little extreme because you may only pop a few beads of sweat due to your inability to FOCUSSSSSS).

Evaluate when you accomplish things and make rational decisions. Aren't you always in a good place with your thoughts and thinking very clear? Even the most grounded person will lose all sense of logic when their thoughts are running away to China. I have been told that I am scaring-ly (new word) calm because I very rarely raise my voice or lose control over my inner expressions. I do not feel super human by maintaining that, I just always think one step ahead of everyone around that is skating up the wall, only to end up right back in front of the same issue that lit them on fire in the first place.

Well how do you handle losing your keys A.D.? Wow, interesting words and questions you have today. I simply slow down to an immediate stop, mentally and physically, and then I evaluate my tracks from start to finish. It is very simple; I move to a neutral point that is familiar but will not distract me and I rewind my most recent steps. To do things in that way, I HAVE TO clear out any extra thoughts from the sidebar of my mind. No need in panicking because the keys are in the house somewhere. Realizing that, I say a little prayer and almost immediately, I find the keys.

I know this was just irrelevant reading about keys to those of you that don't process that way of thinking, but if you can grasp an understanding, it's about much more than that. Why go crazy over things that still need closure? Why continue to practice the same behavior that has gotten you nowhere fast? It is all about remaining centered in your own world so you can be healthy and happy with no additives. When your thoughts are disturbed by an uproar you refuse to let die, it stops you from approaching things with a peaceful mind. So what, you and your mate are fussing; who says you have to yell back? What point does that make? Oh, you can scream louder??? Makes sense now. And of course your boss yelled at you so why not turn in your resignation or JUST QUIT!!!! I have two theories in life; fix it or shut-up. Whining doesn't fix anything unless you're 2 years old and adults need to figure out what's wrong with you. Once you have faced a situation and even let off the steam of it truly tearing up your last good nerve (y'all know how it is or is that just me?), let it go and handle yo bidness!!!!! (Had to take it there for those that think small, lol)

All in all, practice stopping yourself when your anxiety takes off. Start thinking about the journey or task with the fact of how silly you will feel once you have lost your cool and still not solved a thing. I am telling you, when you are the one with clarity in any situation but things and others around you are still spinning, you will always have the better answer and definitely you will win any argument.

"I've been hurt in my life & developed trust issues from the pain, but I must say, God has made up for all of that w/ folks close to me now."

A.D. Whittington

Revisions of Life

I guess the desire to be a better person is something racing through minds across America but sometimes the efforts seem to differ. Everyone talks about doing things and becoming great, getting ahead and finding their pot of gold, but what actions are displayed with all this hard work of "nothing"? I listen to glamorous tales about having a great business or finding the perfect mate but all I see is channel flipping in your mind and never any real movement off the couch.

I have high hopes and dreams with my writing and utilizing my ability to give positive energy to the world. I have come to terms with the fact my life is destined to help others and I must make all my brain power work in the direction going forward instead of lying still on a rock. Nothing is ever gained without footwork and evaluation to calculate better results my friend.

You say you need a job and nobody will hire you? I guess if I laid there all day I would get that answer too because the psychic part of my mind has gathered database from all over the city leading me to the ranch in this fantasy I created. I'm not telling you that you will get the perfect job just because you try, but the lazy bug needs to be terminated by a burst of mental fire powered by your desires and motivation. You want things but refuse to make any efforts in a direction to gain. If things you do now aren't working but you stay on a ragged road that tears up your tires and throws off your alignment, why in the world are you complaining about the failures???

I have the most confused look on my face when someone tells me they wish they could find the perfect mate but they continue to stay in a relationship with the perfect package of misery. You wish they would stop cheating you say? You're shocked they keep using you even though you love them? Did I just hear you say they keep embarrassing you even though you repeatedly tell them that hurt? Wow, I can see why you're supposed to gain a better future with solid companionship, you're doing everything right, according to you. HA! Wake up man! You are planted in the sewer but tried to order roses and got ticked off when the florist said they won't deliver to that area. Are you kidding me?? Of course not, and as you read you think I'm tripping right now.

There are signs in life we need to shift the routine around and take a path we see around that corner. Comfort level is easy to settle with but that's not the key for excellence, it's just what becomes normal to avoid real thinking. I look at the mind as a car; you must do proper maintenance to stay mobile. If you put dirt in the gas tank and sugar in the engine, you're not gonna get far dude, and the smoke that will cloud right before the explosion might kill you. Rotate those tires, and when they are worn, replace them. Invest in products that have reliability and nice warranties so you can be more prepared for disaster. Once you reach the point that car isn't appropriate for you anymore or it keeps giving you trouble, stopping you from doing ANYTHING, it's time to upgrade and trade.

No need in poking your lip out about the terrible feeling you hold deep in your soul, it's your fault it has leeched on and refuses to move. Drink something like fruitful knowledge and positive energy; all that worthless energy will leave faster than a prostitute at a house being raided by the police. You must like your failures because each time a plane or monster vehicle (positive people, healing from hurt, glorified revelation in self) tries to rescue you, I see you wave it away with excuses and whining, always trying to justify but you're the only one that believes the foolishness.

There is nothing different to expect if you don't do something that breaks the cycle in your personal space. I am sending some positive energy with forces of strength to carry in your pocket; it's a tough mission but definitely one that is attainable. Be excited for gaining truth with promise, not just a good talk that sounds like Charlie Brown's teacher *wahwahwahwahwah WAHH WAHHH!!! Rejoice with your victory, it is something that is guaranteed to be refreshing and everlasting.

"I don't really care who doesn't like me or has negative thoughts concerning any part of my existence; I'm not here seeking approval."

It's My Fault....

"You're aware of the damages your current situation holds, it's your job to change the setting if you truly want different results."

A.D. Whittington

Helplessness

So that everyone is on the same page, I want to start from the beginning. In the years that processed long before I was thought of, men were the head of the household and did everything in their power to assure their family was supported properly. If they had to walk long distances to and from, they held legitimate jobs and assured security for their wife and children. Nothing was too dangerous and there was no such thing as a woman doing anything manual other than "helping"; simply assisting the husband with his primary duties, every now and again. You would never see a man leaving his responsibilities on anyone much less neglecting his home. I am almost certain those tragic things happened constantly but it wasn't enough to notice or make a difference.

Men were raised to be polite and treat women with nothing but respect. They wouldn't dare ask a woman for money and it was unheard of for a woman to take on the burdens of household finances. Love was love and everything in between just kept the family strong. I remember witnessing my friend's uncle lose his job and all he ever said was "I refuse to lose my family so I have to make sure I keep a roof over their head. We will not go live with our parents because this is my family and I am responsible for making sure they remain stable".

Now let's go to present day America; where things are supposedly progressing and women of this country have more freedom compared to other nations. We may have grown in the sense of less prejudice values, but we are still stuck in a time warp of pitiful females. It is worse today than it ever could be. I am so embarrassed at the number of women allowing men to rule their minds and overall comprehension of daily living. I am not judging those women; I just do not understand their thought process. Maybe they feel they are not worthy of being spoiled or treated with the utmost respect; to include being financially stable with their dominant mate.

This topic expands over into the LGBT (Lesbian/Gay/Bi/Transgendered) community as well. Women want to play the "male" role but they are not taking charge and handling their situations in the way a real "man" should. It doesn't make you a real "man" just because you are employed unless you budget correctly and always make sure your family doesn't go without the necessities in life. I believe strongly in the old fashion values of working and providing. This is 2012 and women share the load because they have just as much knowledge as men. There should not be a man or wo"man" on this earth that is okay with their feminine mate being in a situation of instability. No woman should have to be at home with her parents, or their mate's, unless you are the victim's of the economy and the bad circumstances that can sometimes brings. Even then, there should be no comfort zone until independence from the temporary trials has been resolved.

Why do women allow men to feed off of their energy but never require him to contribute? Why is it okay that a couple stay with his or her family because he has not taken the initiative to find a place they can call their own? Why in the world is he ok with not being the true "MAN OF THE HOUSE" because he has allowed himself to stay in a position of contentment under another person's shelter and constant rule? These are all questions that have no real answer.

There will never be clarification on this issue because there will always be a woman that feels she NEEDS that worthless man to validate her inner spirit. Tsk tsk and shaking my head at the standards that are accepted by women everywhere.

BE THANKFUL

It doesn't take a complex mind or list of extended vocabulary words to give thanks. Do not spend your day complaining about all that doesn't exist or feels wrong, this is reality of life. When opening our eyes each day, we take for granted the blessing in the fact we exist, another chance to be more than we attempted the day before. I can give you simple love and desires for going forward, be a solid rock for small things and overwhelmed with joy for beautiful leaps and bounds. I am grateful for each and every one of you, the motivation of your presence drives my energy level into a place you are reading about right now. I want to grow and be a balance of true understanding for connected hearts that came here as one. Thank you for the arrival of your zone and recycle this for all to feel...

"Just because somebody did or said something you don't like doesn't mean they're not a good person, it just means they upset you. No need in speaking in negative terms & trying to make them look bad to win sympathy votes, your personality should draw folks close to you, not a pity party."

Everybody either knows someone that is guilty of the above or this post is for you directly. It's straight to the point; just because you're upset you don't need to talk junk. The things I witness in life when people get mad is humiliating and it's not even happening to me. I can never understand how things were so perfect but because there was a disagreement, foul words start flying and it's time to pull out swords and shields. People are best friends but when they fall out, that 'bleepity-bleep-bleep-ain't-bleep'. Yes what they did was wrong but what are you trying to accomplish by posting negative things all over your social networking site? Are you trying to humiliate them or just see how much you can embarrass yourself? Seriously? You still didn't solve anything, only keeping a fire going that is being fueled by toxic gasoline ready to explode in your face. I have seen folks get other people to help them fight and we all know that is weakness at it's finest. If you can't battle by yourself you might not want to keep involving yourself in crucial situations. Don't even pick up the phone and start the freight train moving, that's between you and another person; all those people getting involved shows how ignorant and afraid you are. Nobody should need attention that bad and you're no exception. I know you won't admit it but it's a fact and the people that allow their existence to be drawn in need a spiritual and mental check as well, that's not your business, plain and simple. Let's not forget the folks you didn't do anything wrong to but they get mad because you have a mind of your own and they retaliate by spreading rumors and lies. Those are my favorite folks because I realize they are extremely weak and that's their only method of "fighting". Real solutions require too much thinking and because their brain doesn't operate on that level, it's an impossible function. If you're the victim of these things, ignore it and dust your shoulders off because you are so important, you have caused levels of the universe to get out of whack. If you're guilty of it, STOP!!!! I don't have any other advice for you besides that, you should know better. Try dealing with life and confronting things to get an honest solution unless you're content showing the world just how lost you are and just how small your brain really is.

Treadmill Mentality

Why in the world do people continue to complain about things they refuse to change? You are probably tired of reading about it but there are so many different ways and angles to approach that topic, I'm just rolling with the obvious things half of you might never even have thought of. In life, we can't do the same things in a fashion that's exact and expect everything to evolve differently. When reaching for new goals, the pattern of thinking must drastically change. I have never seen a store keep the same amount of inventory for extended periods of time and aggressively order new items before clearing out the old space with moneymaking results. You start to see mega sale signs appear or a re-design in features to attract a mass quantity of quality customers while moving the old out, phasing in fresh merchandise.

Check the price tags of your spirit and see if you in fact are running in place and vigorously reaching for the cheese tied to the string at the end of the stick. Are you forming realistic agendas to progress forward or do you feel that one day you're going to get that rap career off the ground from the studio planted in your mama's basement? You're 40 man, give it up!

I watch the faces of defeat and hear people's cries of sorrow. I evaluate the energy that doesn't change, but yet these same people let anger explode about all that's wrong in the situation; refusing to accept any responsibility for the damage. Running in place is not a bad thing, but be aware that the sweat you're fumigating the room with is now old and stale. How about circulate the air and process a new method of running to your destiny? The routine you refuse to adjust is the same routine you will remain stuck in for eternity.

"Some of you need to cut a lot of negative energy loose, being attached to other human beings isn't that important and it eventually affects your spiritual existence. Negative and positive can't exist in the same setting, stop trying to justify reasons simply because you don't want to hurt someone's feelings. When the journey is over, your stability is all you can account for."

A.D. Whittington

Fresh Air

Everybody has strived to achieve victory with his or her accomplishments. From learning to walk to figuring out how to balance a checkbook, there are no perfect starts to last a lifetime. No such thing as processing a flawless picture of who we are, that's an impossible task and will never be true of anyone. I know my growth came from years of messing up with my life and finally one day; I woke up and made the choice to be more productive. I have no room to talk about others because their life is off track, but I will speak of pushing forward for a better tomorrow, feeling as one because I was once at the bottom of thinking great things about my prosperity.

I have blown my money and not paid a bill, only to come home and see the electric company didn't agree with my negligent behavior. Now I am sitting in the dark with nothing to show except a hangover that has gone on for days. Is there a lesson in that? Of course there is; make sure you prioritize what is important. Being helpless means you are confused and blind, not ABLE to see the light of a better path but when we continue down the same road that circles around to the same point every single time, it's now time to change directions.

Our job as leaders and individuals that are aware is to help others, not hinder with overwhelming views too hard to understand. If you have bounced from the low pits and now sit in a position to network with positive energy, teach others how to crawl before walking in the struggles to resolve. Will everybody jump on and become a pro in a day? Definitely not, but you must lead an approachable life and invite the lost into your population of comfort. Be mindful that you were once in a lonely walk of disbelief and had to wake up in a daze, without a clue of how you would make it another day. Be giving of love and thoughts; have enough patience to know everyone will grow at a different speed because there should be no rushing when it's not the appropriate time. Once you know in your heart you genuinely assisted with new visions, be at ease letting the bird fly out of the cage. Make sure you do not slander and disgrace those less knowledgeable, that never helps, it only hurts and puts a wedge with the big reality.

For those of you that are lost, you must take pride and responsibility in your efforts first and foremost. Stop making excuses and make attempts. You know right from wrong, and if you're still stuck at the starting point years later, it is now evident that you are content right where you are and nobody can make you motivate out of there, except you. The old saying "actions speak louder than words" does really mean a direct message. You can talk a good game but if you are still doing the same thing, why should others take you serious and why are you so upset they have no faith in you? Evaluation time applies to all that are functioning; no progress will be made without looking inside and throwing out a lifeline of hope and desire.

Be united and help all that will receive. Never force your love or views onto a closed mind, just remain true with what you attempt in life.

"When you know your worth, other folks opinions will never tarnish the reality of your heart #priceless"

A.D.Whittington

When do I really matter?

I am sitting here in deep thought about the way my life has transformed at different times along my journey. From early days, I was subject to being teased and bullied, never understanding the value of people that would actually be important to my future. I didn't know how to build healthy friendships with those in my age group, so I was a constant outcast among my peers.

I can look at the pain that lingers in people's eyes because they have been abandoned or rejected all their life, and I fully understand how that wound can hold you hostage. Friendship is something very rare to find, and having the support of others will be a topic that you keep as a priority in your heart during steady balance. I used to want the popular crowd to embrace me and chant my praises while I entered the halls of school. I would sit and watch everyone who received thunderous response when they stepped on campus and envy their stride. Boy, the lucky ducks they were, always in the top fashion and rolling with the best.

I went through young adulthood wanting my world to be in a direction of shine, so I thought. I didn't realize that people are human just like me and without my own inner strength, I would never be included in activities; I couldn't even see myself in a great light. I was confused about my purpose and had to wrap my thoughts around the point of still being thrown to the side. I cried and had hurt feelings because my "friends" only damaged my reputation and drove a stake through my soul with their taunting, not giving those warm interactions to make my spirit smile.

I took some time to find me. I finally got to the point that I could look at my reflection and notice how great I am. The glowing picture I started to see was erasing the cloudy film of dismay that often times overpowered the scene. I had the revelations of my existence, standing in the mirror often just to gaze at this beautiful person with a strong voice; attracted to the greater good of life. I filtered out having folks around just to take up space and I bottled up all the anger and fear that kept me in a hostile state. Once I believed in my ability to be an asset in my solo career, I became united inside and super glue held the hope together, fusing it to concrete prosperity. I learned I could demand what helps me and I had the power to refuse any energy that wasn't sufficient for sustaining a concrete relationship with my magnificent self. I didn't NEED to be "in" to be meaningful, only solid with my own recognition of my charming individuality.

I pursue many areas in life and I have finally conceived the basics of pure and innocent friendship, no strings attached and no conditions to participate. I look to those that I truly matter to and consistently uphold me during difficult times. I no longer NEED others to feel complete; I started to choose only certain energy to interact with me on a constant movement. When I am tracking forward, I want to share my rewards with those who are simple and possess love from the heart, amounting to confident feelings of security as resolution. If you can't be a root during the crawl, I will be even further disconnected once the tree is done blooming. I don't require much, just true clarification of honesty and the recycling of trust and love I give. I definitely require support, simply because of the importance I place on ventures I seek. I have refined my mentality of what makes me feel elevated in quality, just simply savoring in the authenticity of who I am.

"I am so disappointed in the choices people continue to make for things they already know are failures. If you stay in the same spot, don't complain about not reaching new heights, it is not humanly possible to go forward while remaining planted in old cement. #breakthechains"

"It's amazing how important you become to people when they realize you are headed toward success. Just because I know you and we get along doesn't mean you are placed in the arena of importance in my life; that spot is currently filled by individuals that have always invested love and constant support for the life I pursue"

A. D. Whittington

Become independent for personal success.....

I process reality with things I have actually witnessed or experienced. Never will I speculate and try to put my stamp on anything I have not sat through, whether it's in the tornado of sorrow or the rain of victory. Life gives all levels of existence, you just have to grab a ticket and know which train to ride. When that is confusing due to lack of understanding, the best teacher is effort and recording the outcome for future actions with lessons learned.

Independence is one of those baskets you jump in that will reveal a lifetime of truth once you embrace the concept of its reality. The beauty of gaining rewards because you set the track in the correct motion makes your heart glow with the boost of accomplishment. To know that you are capable of success by putting forth the right thought process and obtaining random goals with diligence shoots you up on the scales of enlightenment. I know how it tears your mind up to depend on others, only to find they are lacking a true connection to sincere giving and not expecting anything in return. They now have the upper hand to throw their "power" and "control" up in your face, observing your every move based on the fact that you need them. I know we all need others to be there and help boost our movement, but it is imperative that we all learn the art of being independent. Only obligated to someone because you want to, not because you have to. To avoid control of your personal space, make sure you have your own living quarters. Save your money or find a great no money down program so your name sits on the line of "OWNER" when signing for your car.

None of these small things come overnight but they are within reach. If you take the focus off others and see deep into your own heart, you can build with small blocks to bust the chains on your restrictions. You should long for the chance to form your own footsteps leading to the break through of positive light. Stop wanting and prepare to start doing. Instead of going out with friends to get drunk or have a good time, put aside money from every check, designating it solely for moving, a car or whatever has you handicapped and isolated. You can't go out to lunch every time folks from the office take off; you have to eat noodles or a sandwich to set your priorities in motion. And why in the world are you buying a new cell phone when the one you have works just fine? I know you like the new design, but come on; you are sleeping on someone's couch and answering calls that ultimately have no privacy. Oh, I know they fall over you and your sexy style, they would definitely think you are a catch if you put that money toward your own ride to work instead of being dropped off.

I very rarely NEED anyone to do things for me; I set my life up that way. I hate having to feel like I owe something just for getting help and I despise having it thrown up in my face. Most people do things JUST to be able to have a slight choke on you, thriving off the fact you are at their mercy. I keep income so I can maintain my monthly bills, sitting down to budget according to the basic necessities. I separate what is a must versus 'ooohhh that's cute and I just want it'. Sometimes I have to get help with things but it's not something I enjoy. I like knowing I strive hard to be honest and devoted to my success because I made it my primary goal. I am not talking down completely about NEEDING anyone because I am above it; I just learned a long time ago you couldn't depend on anyone but yourself all the time for everything. If you get in the practice of making a successful path alone, whether folks are reliable or against the flow, you won't suffer and everything you ever need will land in your lap based on your strength and true independent agenda.

Right is right......

I live in the same world that the rest of you call life. I encounter diversity in all forms, not always pleasant or settling, but necessary. I am excited about the things that are swept under the rug because folks don't want to step on toes or cause a room full of people to gasp while covering their mouth in astonishment; bold is my main avenue for delivering the messages of balance. I am not a literary bully; I am just very direct with my communication of reality. Why pretend like things need to be "left alone" because it's routine and just flat out normal? Yeah right, that doesn't make it correct, it just makes it something that hasn't been the centerpiece of the table and the rest of the world is too lazy to look in the dark corner to put up a fight for a better society in the mental health department.

Now that I took the train around the corner to enjoy the scenery instead of jumping straight across the tracks to land at my destination, I am really wide open with no brakes on the cart, WHOOOO!!!!! I know that the world still has warped views of "how it's supposed to be" with men and women in these pre-defined roles from centuries ago, but I am over it. I am so liberal it isn't even funny, and not just pro woman, I am pro common sense. I'm sure that men everywhere would love nothing more than a planet full of Stepford Wives (maybe not all of you but you are the few that actually make life glorious when other creatures talk with you). If you have two adults that are consenting to all choices, the brain cells or gender don't even matter, the fact that it's legal and agreed upon equally outweighs any outside opinions.

Girl meets boy. Girl likes boy. Girl gets really hyper when boy's name comes across the caller i.d. for their date. Girl dresses beautiful. Girl waits on boy to arrive and sweep her off her feet. Girl gets in car and loves the great date. Girl invites boy back to her place because all this romancing made her inside feelings rage out of control. Girl asks boy if he has condoms, because if he doesn't, she practices safe interactions on an intimate level and has her own. Girl allows boy to approach her intimately and girl is now in heightened ecstasy with same boy who is ready to show his side. (AND ACTION!!!!) S/N: this is going to get long but I want the whole date to be a movie from beginning to end, but since this is a book and not a comic strip rolling with visuals~~~>HERE WE GO!!! Boy meets girl. Boy reallllly likes girl and can't wait to "score"; so who's easy now? Come on; look at how early he was thinking about hanky-panky in his script. Yeah, I know, it's okay that you just recognized it, that's why I'm writing. Before the date, boy calls close female friend for pointers on how to reach his final goal. Boy takes shower and splashes great smelling cologne on every region of his body. Boy drives to pick up girl with the notion he wants to have sweaty lingo at the end of the night (MESSAGE!!!!) but if she's "easy" he will never see her again (and this is where the ignorant and contradicting myth throws me OFF the bus, he just categorized her as easy even though he is plotting on his final move before he leaves home~~~>MESSAGE!!!). Boy takes girl to a beautiful setting and boy wines her until she melts. When girl wants to go back to her place later, boy gladly takes the invite because boy wants girl more than he can stand but boy still passes judgment of what he will think when girl agrees to have an intimate moment too soon but boy doesn't have condoms so boy feels disappointed but boy becomes extremely turned off when girl pulls out the same size box boy owns for his occasional spontaneous lust filled sprouts. BOY!!!! That was quite a bit but very necessary to create. Personally, I am done fooling with him because all that just gave me a serious headache and left me no room for anything else from him or his camp. Hmmmmmmph!!!!

You can read that again if you got lost but it looks like they both wanted to have some type of physical contact when the night started, but 'girl' is living outside the box that doesn't even exist, just some stupid chalk lines the ancestors set forth when that's all they had to work with, literally. Who is wrong here? No seriously, she was being "fast" and giving it up on the first night when she SHOULD be following the recycled thoughts of people dead and gone and keep herself away from physical temptation. He can feel a certain way but she better decline and hold that feeling until it's official; smothering her insides to be submissive and give in to his manhood and her bursting flame at "the right time". Bull'ish man, I am so over that whole talk about women being "loose" simply because they happen to want what men want. Yes, I said it and that's where I stand. I am very outspoken and concrete with my views of how society poisoning your brain with nonsense controls the way you look sideways toward the lady sitting in front of you at church because she had relations with your arrogant brother last night. She didn't force him and didn't even have to verbalize her want before he ripped his zipper and tripped over the couch hopping to her "rescue". Get a life and sit yo' 'gossip-driven-no-real-excitement-based-life-so-you-meddle-everywhere-else' self down. NOW!

I am not promoting one nightstands or intimacy on the first date; I personally have never experienced that in life because of my values. I choose to wait until I build something concrete with one individual, but in reality, the above scenario is going to always happen in America if I never ever wrote another word. I am pushing fair and diverse thinking into your lap because that mess you have been chewing on is worse than old gum. Welcome to the world of beautiful lights, where you tell the doctor the truth about your daily routine and you don't lie to impress him; he is going to run test and find that lard around your heart, so just write down the tacos you eat everyday right before your three Krispy Kreme doughnuts. It feels great to be free of irrelevant bondage; I am so hyped for your fresh start and proud of your ability to accept your responsibility in this bonfire.

"Ok, maybe I'm just getting old & "not cool" anymore, but my mind thinks that priorities in life are more important than random things that don't matter. How is it ok to have new rims but your lights are off, fresh clothes but your child needs diapers, partying all weekend but no gas to get to work? The list of confusion is much longer, those are just a couple highlights."

A.D.Whittington

Mommy Dearest....

The definition of mother is: *a*: a female parent *b (1)* : a woman in authority; *(2)* : an old or elderly woman that has maternal tenderness or affection. Houston, we have a problem!!! Not an issue of women taking that position, but a huge disaster when they don't fill those shoes to the max. Yes, I am going to hit on the population of sorry baby mamas. Man, this is going to be a good one; I need toes to be stepped on and spirits to rattle because the disgrace is overwhelming.

This particular topic, like so many others, irritates the ba-jee-bees out of me. I can speak on everything I write about with clear understanding but this one does something to my soul y'all. It punches me in the stomach and makes my head pop off (yeah, all that). I am a living and breathing woman who gave birth to a child. I didn't steal him or adopt him; he was pushed out into the world through natural methods; although I did receive drugs to assist with pain control because the contractions were a beast! Whew, I started sweating just thinking about it. Having a baby is something serious, there's no substitute for the experience, only comparison of horrifically (not even sure that's a word, lol) devastating moments of an out of body shock. I am sure you're reading this and trying to figure out what in the world it has to do with the intro, but trust me; it leads you to the door opening into reality.

I know that the world looks at bad fathers and trashes their image because they can be slack, but it really turns somebody's head when a mother is absent financially or otherwise. We will definitely use the term 'deadbeat' to attach with that description, and the breakdown follows, so calm your nerves and stop explaining yourself ma'am. I have never been able to understand how it comes to the point ANY woman can give birth to a human being and pass responsibility to someone else's lap. I'm not talking about the females who have their children and life makes it impossible to raise them so a family member or close friend steps in to make sure the child has stability; life happens and it's better for the child to be safe than struggle. I am talking about the women who know that family member or friend is raising their child but they don't do anything to assist financially. I know the economy is tough, but you have to fight tooth and nail for something to give with support. That word (support) is a basic necessity that should just happen without hesitation, but it seems to be put on the back burner for some. Nobody is passing judgment on you for not having physical custody, but why in the world do you have peace at night NOT giving your extra money and time? You need to be there to give some feedback with your child; going by every few weeks doesn't put you in the column of 'Parent of the Year'. What about the women who never get a break from their child (ren)?

There are not opportunities to just pass them off for days at a time; the obligation of daily nurturing is a priority. Every time I meet someone who I see in the spotlight of life on a regular basis, hosting parties, clubbing three to four nights a week, having wonderful alcohol sessions with their friends, shopping endlessly for the latest shoes and handbags or anything else that has them "running the streets" as my grandmother can say, I automatically assume they are single with no kids. Imagine when I find out they have given birth one to three times, if not more, but they don't have the child (ren) with them because they can't afford to take care of them? You sure fooled me that you're broke, I see the budget you have set for yourself, you just can't afford to raise them and still maintain all that good stuff you are used to. Reality check, sacrifice is included in that oath you took when you decided to have consenting intercourse and you came up pregnant; there's no free pass just because you have someone to 'help' you out. That's so selfish, and in my mind, I automatically feel pain for the kids. They are not connected with the most important line of love, the originating umbilical cord for their every breath, their mom. Yes dads are important, but these spawned human beings were made inside you, how can that just be a thought in the back of your mind that comes up on occasions?

Now you know if I touched on the fact you're absent in different capacities, I am furious when

I see the mother looking wonderful and the kids look like they don't have anywhere to call home. That disgusts me with a serious rage, the ultimate form of being selfish. That dirty diaper needs to be changed, but when you call someone to borrow money because after you left the salon and hit up the mall for that party you attended last night that had admission of $20 a person and created a drink tab of $60, you got an attitude because you can't even purchase baby wipes or milk and people you are calling paid their bills so they don't have any extra money to spare for your personal responsibilities. Are you kidding me??? Clearly you're not and this is what you're used to doing.

The fact that you depend on a check from the state or a man that refuses to comply with court orders displays your true lack of desire to do things for your kids. All the extra funds is great, and definitely helps, but you must make it clear in your life walk that your kids will be taken care of no matter what the days and months hold. Then some women that are fortunate enough to receive timely child support from the fathers go and blow the whole thing on their personal wants. It's not yours, that's why it's called CHILD support, to assist with taking care of the child. To assist means to add to what you do already, but you wouldn't know about that since you don't move a finger in that department. You should be embarrassed reading this because it's tragic for others to watch, I am embarrassed for you.

Who cares that you're tired of being single so you have to spend so much extra money to get jazzy and go to the club in search of a good baby daddy? Focus on the task at hand, being a better mother. My blood is boiling as I type and I'm going so fast, trying to get it out, I keep stumbling over letters. I'm here to let you know that the act should be retired. I heard you aren't selling many tickets to the drama fest of neglect, so please sit down and learn how to be more effective in your kid's life. If you feel like you just don't know so therefore you don't even try, research some help groups and talk to someone; stop letting helpless souls that rely on you for everything suffer because you have self-esteem issues and want to win the battle of being the best in life in every area except with your precious offspring. News flash ma'am, you are really low on the pole of reality, no purpose is ever coming and blessings can't be retrieved for longevity until you turn completely around in the middle of the road. You went through a love-starved childhood, so now the babies you made because you refuse to close your legs have to take all the hits, only to keep the cycle going for many years. I am like pesticide for the roaches and insects of your mind, terminating and killing ALL that toxic thinking you manage to let be your way of life. Please stop making excuses and really take a look at the problem, only you control what you pursue, and right now, it can only include the biological and genetic image of what you gave life.

Good men can be hard to find.

I like to ask people what their thoughts are on life. It makes me more aware of what is really happening in folk's brain, other than my own. You have to be able to process different subjects to say you thoroughly connect with others, and that is my key reason for what you're reading. I refuse to remain ignorant but portray that I know everything, because I don't. I happen to know a lot and it is credited to my ability to open my mind and understand the differences that exist in the world. I don't always have the experience I hear of but I try my best to make sure I listen for fair evaluation.

I posted a random topic on my social networking site and I got quite a few responses from men and women. I love that people want to speak about what lies in their heart, that's the only way we can bridge the gap on diversity. A young man that said he is disturbed about good men not being recognized more touched my heart. I know I am not a father, husband, brother or any other type of male, but I know exactly what he's talking about. I can relate and it makes sense from another point of view, regardless of what I will ever know first hand with this particular topic.

There are so many points of interest to recognize mother's of the world, but the male population usually only gains a voice when they're being talked about in a negative way. They are living at home with their mama, they're being released from prison and running the streets in the drug game, trying to juggle multiple women or just plain out doing nothing positive with their life. I know those things exist in abundance but that's not fair for those who do the right thing on a regular basis. I get it, I would be ticked off too if I was grouped in with a bunch of losers, knowing good and well I am disgusted by their slack ways just like the rest of the world. Mother's Day is a HUGE event in almost everyone's life; stores do all types of special promotions to approach this big day of making women everywhere feel special. I watch television and see commercials reminding you months in advance, scared that the women in your life will be left in the cold. They do some promotion for Father's Day, but it is very rare you see parades as the focus of the wonderful men who deal with life and still make their home with wife and kids a normal task on a day-to-day basis. I have to evaluate my own participation in the neglect of the good men of the world; I want to be in the number of making the silent voice of all their efforts ring loud.

We are all responsible for being more active with giving a better view of men; talking a good game never won anything without the steps going forward being planted firmly at the line. It is a sad occasion that bad outweighs good, but pointing a finger while claiming to push victory will not give full gratification. Good men deserve to know how important they are in society and in the lives of those they touch directly.

Your actions speak volumes of ignorance....

I just don't understand how this world remains so lost in the cycle of blind acceptance. I'm not being arrogant about the fact I'm a great writer when I tell you that I need everybody to direct others to this book so we can all be on one accord with becoming more productive as a nation. I watch so much go on around me and because I used to be a sad puppy with no bone to chase, I can spot the clues a mile away. I like to consider myself a pretty cool person, outside of writing and communicating online; I carry the same direct personality if we had a conversation in the parking lot of Wal-Mart. I keep my mind in a solid state of honest behavior and I ALWAYS take responsibility for my actions, even my negative effects on situations in the world.

I am baffled with the people who are confused when things in life don't go right and they constantly blame others. When I am listening to a story, I like to rewind the time in my mind and piece together all the possible options. It's even worse when I know for a fact that someone is playing the victim and pretending like nothing they did is to blame for horrible results they encounter and experience. I'm not going to tell you to try and be better in life so things will look up and the magic just happens with no work on your end. This is the blow to your chest that pokes you straight through the lung, forcing you to scream out words of honesty, finally.

If you are running around like the world continues to do you wrong but in true focus, your initial actions made the storm come, sit down and stop talking. You know good and well that you are not innocent, pushing everything to the front door while you slide out the back. Remember, it was you that set this movie in motion, directing and producing the tragedy you have been trying to run from but feel so connected to. Stop looking confused because things keep popping up, you're the one that won't leave well enough alone. Are you upset that nobody is tuned into your station anymore? Your network doesn't provide quality programming but you keep trying to force viewers attention toward what you are doing; it's still not very enlightening by the way.

I can never quite grasp the thought process behind victimized thinking. It just makes my jaw drop that folks really have a mind that doesn't understand the sand storm flying around them. It is amazing how the memory deletes the early events that start the drama. Yes, the drama boo, that's just what it is. I can't allow you to feel that what you have been doing for years is okay because frankly it's nerve wrecking. We see you and we all know, at least the logical portion of the population, that you're full of it. We know what you did many moons ago that is just now settling but continuing to drag fragments that linger at the center of attention. I'm glad you have moved on but you created this forest fire that you can't get to die out completely. Then you don't even have the maturity to let the dead dogs lie; you poke and push with any "hidden" chance you get. Yeah, we see that too. You act like you're tired but you must miss the antics in some form or fashion because you show jealousy and rage every chance you get. You only make sense to yourself and those around you that you've convinced you are oh-sooo-innocent. I know how you do, you have to build your bandwagon because you're far from honest and if it was completely revealed to every person that encounters you, you would be dead upon sight.

So let's start being real and stop skipping around like you're this big eyed puppy dog that was picked up by animal control for nothing, but in reality, you ate through 6 people's garden and destroyed everything in your path before lying down in the pasture to take a nap; the net is coming down and you gotta go.

Connecting with harmony

The worst mistake that exist in America is the smaller picture of bright lights. The billboards read that we should all behave one way but in reality, there is no true rulebook to follow. The only requirement is to do the right thing and make the heart happy according to experiences. I can never tell another person what to do, I can only share my views, but those views won't always work for every single person that I interact with or give insight to. It all depends on where you stand in your pool of survival. I enjoy sharing the ways I function and expressing what I have found to be the general flow of moving but I am not the last stop on the train. I live each second of my growth to help someone else learn a different approach. Notice I said different because it's not the only way, it can only be used to relate and familiarize for a comfortable ride. Life is scary and when you feel lost and alone, it is torture to endure. I will never be able to "fix" every possible flaw that every human being has or goes through, but I pray I can contribute to some beautiful relief in the relaxed vibe of your soul.

"No matter how close I am to someone, if another human being trust me enough to vent or seek advice about that someone, I will hold it dear & realize they're just venting, not gossiping, so I respect it as such. Everybody has emotions & needs somebody they can trust to talk to without having their intimate thoughts of the heart repeated #fact"

A.D.Whittington

I guess I will never understand how people can walk around for weeks, days or even hours giving miserable vibes with just breathing. It's not the rest of the world's fault that there is something out of whack so why in the world do you think it's fair to just fly off the handle at innocent individuals? I know you're aggravated but I didn't do anything except speak. That barking you're doing that has taken you into the dark halls with no light is not what I was looking for when we connected on sight. I need to be honest when talking to you all because I will never claim to be perfect; I always practice what I preach. I can be as moody as the next person but I make sure I manage it within a perimeter of control so it doesn't have to fall in anyone's lap. If I'm skipping around in public or your area of existence yelling and screaming because I spilled my drink, that's not even close to being okay, but if I'm at home and trying to spend time getting my life together in silence, I have a right to demand respect for my personal space.

There are things you can put in your spirit that will keep you from dangling over the pits of horror; they will protect you from the poison that is trying to attack your natural glow. I understand that it becomes a bad day when everything has tumbled into your world, but you don't have to stay there. I already know you want to sit and do nothing, but once you start the pity party, more negative energy jumps right on and doesn't have to fight much to make your life worse. Break your back for your sanity like you do for things that are not going to help you succeed, the extra effort will be utilized for a better today. I hope you take this challenge and captivate the bliss that lies right around the corner.

Power Surge

Let me have 'People Who Thrive on Power and Authority Because They Truly Don't Know the Value of Life' for $200 Alex.

Yes it's true; there are many things to be confirmed by someone who lives their life on a "power trip". Folks who attempt to make their presence known with their "firm" tone and overall body language. Grab your pen and pad to take notes everybody, don't be a victim of the ignorance any longer.

It's sad that some folks are prisoners of their own mind. Always pushing negative energy into a closet they later choose to throw out into the world because they aren't prepared to handle the overload of their own thoughts. You see it everyday; someone walking around with invisible clipboards and holding pens that write in blood, documenting every little thing that goes on in hopes of finding an exit from their own misery. They try and corner their employees with demand and want the intimidation of their "power" to feel threatening. They love to make others sweat but they're secretly processing the value of their thinking, realizing it is too much to handle while breathing in their own skin.

The truth about these lost souls is not that they have the best education in the world or even that they have found unique ways to exhibit their brilliance, my direct experience has shown me that it is the complete opposite. Random people that don't have money or college degrees tend to have more balance and wisdom than the 'Power Crew' simply because the channels the 'Crew' uses on a day-to-day basis has a whole lot of static in the line. They usually have a very unhappy home life, subject to mental or verbal abuse. They are often times being submissive to other people that constantly destroy their spirit behind closed doors. They never get a breath of fresh air in their daily routine so they find zones where nobody knows the reality of who they really are or have a clue about all the suffering they endure in their personal life. When they enter into the workforce or other public setting, they always have to "steal the show", making their "authority" known by sounding off meaninglessly, just to get others to look their way. All the glamour some folks envy is just a cover for the worst emotional pain one person could ever encounter. There are so many examples I could use to highlight the tragedy of their mental confinement but then I wouldn't be able to give you all variety and this book would be all about them, though we all know they would love that.

Things that can wait to be addressed always have to be taken care of at the very moment their insecurity peaks, which is evidently their dominating hunger shifting to high speeds.

I mean, the schedule didn't have to be discussed at this exact second, lunch just started. You waited until folks had their coats on with car keys and small talk in hand to open the discussion, even though you haven't said a word all day. You need to feel like you control things so the best way to show that is to make a big deal RIGHT NOW!!! There, everyone stopped, and even though you aggravated the energy in the room, you got your way~~~>so na-na-ne-boo-boo ugly abandonment issues, VICTORY IS HERE!!! NOT! The pathetic reasons for your personal satisfaction are only driving nails into the wall of dumb things that uplift you. You didn't experience anything fulfilling as a child and based on your clingy love affair with power, you're trying to capture all of that now. Definitely don't keep yourself in the depressing areas of isolation through adulthood, but can you work out the abuse and horrible emotions that have you trapped in the 'Zone-of-Misery' at a more appropriate time for the rest of us?

There is a huge lack of confidence because the point of being "in control" is what they require to feel "pretty". They need to always connect with a higher level of security and if everyone doesn't recognize the power they have finally gained in life, the universe will see a serious meltdown because their mind isn't strong enough to deal with reality. I mean come on man, are you serious? You're so weak that the only people you can tell what to do are folks that need a paycheck or individuals you deem weaker than you? Why are you telling anybody what to do in a degrading way? Life is about respect and it seems that you have none for other individuals. Of course that's the route that's taken, the economy is horrible so nothing negative will happen during your rants of stupidity, but it does display your cowardly ways. Some people become terrified when that person even looks in their direction, but the part that's hidden is, "The Crew" doesn't even know how to tie their own shoes without jacking up natural world order, they just appear to have great control. No need in shaking from fear of the "monster", their mind only has the capacity of an acorn, in the winter.

All their ridiculous yelling and snide remarks only makes them look 12 trying to win a game of chicken on the monkey bars. I want to just hug them because the inner spirit they call their "life" truly sucks dude!!!! Man, it's far from scary, it's annoying to witness the struggle with simply existing; grappling for any little breathe they can unlawfully kidnap to boost their withered confidence.

WRITE THIS ON YOUR BATHROOM MIRROR AND REPEAT IT 100 TIMES A DAY:

"I deserve to receive everything positive that I desire"

Sincerely, (FILL IN YOUR NAME HERE)

You never know until you try...

This is a beautiful moment filled with so many words of expression; I love when people ask my views on random subjects. I state it clear all the time but let me insert my stamp again; I am not licensed in any form, but based on experiences and observations, I have truly been blessed to deal with different levels of negative along with positive energy. Those valuable moments have left me full of racing memories I must put somewhere, so here you sit reading a small portion of my thoughts even though there's so much more where all this came from.

I was having a very in depth conversation with someone about living the best life for the future. I could see pain in their eyes when they expressed how much it would mean to be free from criticism and judgment. I listened closely because everything we exchanged in words led to one place; it is a firm foundation when you have peace for all the choices you make simply because your heart drives you with no regrets. I do know there will be mistakes you want to change and failures you truly wish would just vanish, but the most fulfilling part is you learn from all angles. Simply put, you have to change whatever is stopping you from going in the right flow by never making the same blunder twice; if you focus on that main key, you will be just fine. There will always be people around who cheer you on, but make sure you factor in the elements of destruction. They usually come disguised as friends or loved ones, wanting the best but never giving positive words for what you pursue. Of course you are going to do stupid things and you need a support team to stop you, but what about when you're looking at the bright lights, weighing all things on a scale for balance, you find that it will work for the best because everything else has landed you with nothing, you pull up a chair to think it over very carefully and the only thing you see is flawless growth but the ones "who-love-you-so-much" stick their foot in the door to hold it open slightly, letting bugs and wind in as distractions? Wow, that was a major sentence to overload your brain and so is the feeling you have right now.

I don't know your personal situation but I can guarantee, you deserve some peace. Why do you have to be a victim of mental and verbal abuse just so others can bounce all over your spirit every chance they get? I know they are miserable and sad about their choices, but why is it fair they put rain in your field of sunshine to relieve some of the anguish they despise facing each day? Oh, they have you to poop on and yell at because they know you feel stuck, trapped with nowhere to go. But wait, was that a new job opportunity that opened up in the next town and the potential employer said they will relocate you and help you get set up? Your brain takes off in another direction and your thoughts become scattered immediately. Oh no, I need to stay because I don't have a car and "everyone" says I won't make it without transportation because I don't know anyone there and I will be lost and have to run back anyway. They said I'm going to fail so I guess I should listen and just let that dream go. WHAT!!! NO! Stop right there, pump those brakes and screech to a halt! Look at what you go through now, you live with relatives that talk bad about you being there; the same relatives that are now telling you to stay because you're going to fail when you move (*clearing my throat on that last sentence because it needs to be evaluated closely) and only let you use their car when their mood is right. You already lost a job because you could never get a ride, even though those "supportive" individuals expected to get part of the bill money and groceries plus $50 a week in gas as your part of this living arrangement. Let's not forget, you're not the only person using that car but each time you turn around, you have to be the one to make sure the petro flows straight into the tank. Yeah, I am fired up; I have a steam engine with a massive horn to blow. Enough is enough. You're looking confused because you keep playing through the question "Why in the world would folks that say they love me want to hold me down?" Ask that question a million times and you're still going to be sleeping on their couch, praying you could find a way out but land at a dead end!

I am here today to help you grab the controls of your life and stop letting fear keep you hostage at the mercy of ANYTHING or ANYONE! Whether they mean well or not, nobody can process your true actions and prosperity but who? That's right, you know the routine. Get the mirror and stare at the answer if this is your first time here and you're lost. I do not dance around the obvious words connecting our paths, it can only come one way➔straight and to the point. I know it's scary, why wouldn't it be? All things new will be different, but how do you know it won't work? A-ha! You don't have a clue. You need to start talking to yourself everyday and encouraging your heart, the personal comfort has to start within and remain guarded from the negative fibers floating through the air. You're not stupid, why would you not do well? I mean, look at the folks you rely on now for insight and direction, they can't figure out what's for dinner each day without creating drama. Aren't you tired of that? Of course you are or you wouldn't still be reading, allowing me help you tiptoe over this broken glass. It's very cutting edge and you will bleed slightly, but Neosporin works great. When this is all over, just slap on gauze to stop the red river that will be flowing and let the process begin. In other words, you won't die from some injury and scrapes, everything has a healing time, it's just all about setting your mind in the right moment to endure and get the idea packaged for your own needs. You definitely need to bookmark this spot; I want to be there for every moment of your victory. Look at it as Rocky times 2 in an isolated training. The main character is you, climbing up those stairs to reach the top, holding your hands above your head and barely able to breathe, but you know you made it. **YOU** made it! With every ounce and extra push, **YOU** made it. With all the raggedy and torn feelings you cried about, **YOU** made it.

No matter what others say, shoot for your dreams. As long as it's healthy for you, don't miss the opportunity to blossom. The regrets will be so much worse than any shortness of breath you have from being drained in your mental lungs, just pause and lean on your knees while you re-coop, sipping some water slow to hydrate. Show others you believe in yourself, there's nothing better than a calm focus of just knowing. When you stand up for yourself, you'll be so surprised how everybody automatically starts to respect you and run the other way, coming back with a attitude of acceptance and pure support.

More space that belongs to you; write down your random thoughts.

You don't know me personally but based on what others say, you've formed an opinion & don't like me? Where's your brain again? You can't think for yourself so you're irrelevant anyway."

A.D.Whittington

UP & AWAYYYYYY

(Pull out your self-esteem and let's do work)

I watched the interaction of people passing by as they communicated with each other and I analyzed conversations all around from a distance. Interesting revelations bought me to this place of retreat; the drive into a greater place is assisted by whom you connect with. You definitely have to find your own place of comfort but the worst thing to do is add negative energy into the equation. When you stand solid in life in the right direction, you have to make the deliberate choice to share moments of victory with others who help you feel great about your accomplishments.

When your goals are geared toward success, only other confident individuals can share in that glory with genuine excitement. There are lots of insecurities in life, but watching someone you care about move forward should definitely never be one of them. Make sure you do the best you can daily and you will long to be surrounded by similar beauty.

This is a small piece of advice but I pray it is powerful and absorbed; don't worry about what is going on around you, take care of you. Always keep your self-esteem and confidence cemented to your soul by cherishing your ability to recognize good in the most rare of moments. Moments of effort, moments of shine and moments of everlasting rapture. I don't care that the guy down the street is opening a store just like yours but he isn't you. Nobody shares the things you carry in your mind for being a winner. Nobody can ever replace the shine of your inner star until you give him or her the power switch that can control the emotions driven by your insecurity. Life can't do a lot of damage until **YOU** lose your steady hand with knowing how great you truly are. I want prosperity to override every shadow of doubt and I expect you to keep the cord tucked away in a secret place, making your fears invisible to all others.

External Process

I am a little bothered by the spirits of negative giving. How in the world could giving be negative? Oh, it can definitely go from unrestricted blessings to "doing-this-just-to-throw-it-up-in-your-face" in a matter of sentences or brief situations. I am so aggravated with that last breakdown because giving is supposed to be connected with a genuine heart and soul. If your main purpose is to make yourself feel uplifted by tearing down the mind of those you "help", you should evaluate your purpose in life and saying you love others. This species of humans loves to say they give because they care, but they always crutch on what they have done to justify their yelling and cussing while putting someone else's energy in a dark pit under the sea. There is no valid reason to mistreat others, no matter how much money you have or the social status you carry. Nothing gives you the right to run around doing and saying things disrespectfully to others; with no regard for anyone because you feel you are "owed it". NOT!!! Wake up Gomer, the streets of Mayberry don't truly exist and neither does your logic, or strong lack of.

Do things in kindness and give because you care. I get so tired of folks helping others but when they get mad, they start the parade of things they have done; like that's the only brick they could find to toss. Instead of being an adult and addressing things of concern, they take cheap jabs and degrade someone's spirit; constantly fighting a battle with overwhelming thirsts for adult interaction and resolution. Stop trying to make a point because your mind is stuck in la-la land and come join society. Make honest attempts to balance within reality versus that corner of isolation you banished your soul to for lack of a better location like, I don't know➔LIFE.

I love to give without expectation➔➔➔that's called altruistic behavior ladies and gentleman and there are no strings attached. When I get upset, I don't expect you to give me back what I offered you weeks and months ago. I am not going to plaster your business on social network sites or drop messages in other folk's inbox just to vent and release all I have built up. There are so many other options to fulfill ragged emotions; it might be associated with adult maturity. Try that one on for size! Maybe I just have some very twisted thoughts, but from what I gather, it might be a logical option with cleansing the mind and being pure towards other.

"Some people are so busy being the "victim" in life, they completely miss the reality that they are the problem .No matter what you want folks to believe so sympathy can win you votes (yeah right), the truth is all that really matters when growth is concerned"

It's My Fault....

"A pretty face don't mean jack if your brain doesn't have the same beauty #myopinion"

A.D.Whittington

The Awakening

Hello sunshine!!!! I pray everything is in balance for you and life is beautiful. I come fired up with good words to digest in your spirit. I am going to touch quite a few bad nerves but the processing must begin! I love to see things in life with solid and rational thinking, but being a true friend requires sincere love. The details are very simple, and unfortunately, TRUE friendship is something so rare to find in this lifetime. What makes someone a "true" friend? Is it about the way someone dresses and the car they drive? Oh no, it's about the money that is involved along with fake style. Yes, I have completely looked in the wrong places for what I thought made sense.

Negative on all the above, that's bogus thinking and definitely shows my comedic side; ha-ha, laugh and enjoy the lighter side of things. It is ridiculous and probably the dumbest action ever to see "friends" as people who tell you what you want to hear instead of things that will actually help you grow in life. It's completely over-rated to be 30 years old and think the person that talks about you behind your back and uses you when it's convenient is your true friend. There is no way you are always right and doing everything perfect but constantly achieve nothing in the direction of getting ahead. Your "friends" think you're great but do not offer true balance or opportunity to help you realize how to become a better person when situations occur. They love to party and be "up in your mix", but refuse to point out the wrong you are guilty of repeatedly doing while functioning in life. What great "friends" you have, and you despise or withdraw from appreciating anyone that gives you a straightforward mind.

How dare someone point out the things you do that destroy relationships and friendships? There's no way you are running around hurting folks and it's wrong. Noooooo, you most definitely can't focus on the individuals that mean well versus the noblest "friends" you have but truly lack. I understand and want to direct all the ridiculous thoughts to a central location, this hole in the wall called honesty.

Wake up!!!! You are completely thrown into the rocks of blinding waves and that cycle needs to be broken. Hate me now because I am not going to stroke your false sense of thinking with fabricated butterflies and unicorns. You need to evaluate the priority of where you are headed and anticipate the fall. Now, get up off the ground where you lie because your face is buried deep in the quicksand of illusions you call friendship and beauty. Stop watching and waiting on change but never take the steps in a better direction. Stop expecting magical thunders of light to miraculously blow rays of happiness because that's never going to happen genius. Staying glued to that spot will only keep you in the drab location so stop looking confused when you remain absent from roll call as we all go forward. The span for being a baby is over, it's time to truly find real friends and let the puppet show stay at the library, not the front row of your life.

"If you have a new mate every 3 months that you're madly in love with, I can't take you serious."

It's My Fault....

"In life, all relationships have 'behind the scene' details nobody can process unless they're actually there; form your opinion carefully."

A.D.Whittington

The true meaning of L-O-V-E

I have discovered in life that relationships are built over time. No automatic setting or position to hold, just taking time to mold and nurture and it is definitely an area of profound gravity with a sensitive nature.

I have been blessed to experience the bad things in life so I have comparison points when I receive the good. Emotions and fears all cloud the brain when searching for connections with another human being, but you must learn to skate past the illusions to feel and breathe in the concrete air of love.

Every person on the planet belongs to a bloodline or family. You were given life on a designated day and pushed through the womb of a female that felt an unbearable physical pain but continued the process without an option. Some of you are fortunate enough to be surrounded by folks that share your DNA and remain close to your personal space. You all celebrate holidays and good grades, exchanging joy and sorrow without having to replace absent love. Your family has decided to take the journey by the horns and you are molded into a masterpiece of loving clay. It's a blessing when you are nestled in love and never had to seek outside sources for mental wealth. The folks that say they accept you unconditionally actually know what your bottom looked like in diapers, lol.

I turn the needle of the record in the opposite direction but hear the same song flow from the speakers. I am a firm believer that you do not have to be tied by genetics to be amongst family. It is everyone's quest to be accepted and embraced with unconditional love. A lot of us (that includes me directly) have grabbed the bag of goodies marked **TRUTH** and dumped it on the table; finding people God gave the clear view of devotion and receive showers of unrestricted love into our lives with open arms for eternity.

I feel like you and I have become a family at this point, sharing moments of intimate thoughts with each passing phrase. I cherish honesty and being free with my personality; that's exactly what I do when I give off shots of joy wrapped in authenticity. Thanks for giving me the opportunity to recycle the knowledge I have gained through my own life choices in hopes of helping others that might struggle in some of these same areas as they strive for their mental and spiritual success.

False Documentation

What in the world is being processed in this society we call equal and full of balance? Why do people find it so difficult to be honest and direct when dealing with others? I sit and watch with quiet observation, looking at various personalities develop and grow around me, realizing there are very few adults that give true facts of who they really are.

There isn't a fancy way to put it; **STOP BEING FAKE FOR THE SAKE OF NOTHING**. What is so horrible about you that it's a task to be upfront about details occurring with your life? When lies are the solution, the freedom for people to make choices without disguise is taken away. I have always wanted to be accepted for who I really am, but if I make things up and create a false image, I am definitely making the choice for others. I am then removing the ability to be embraced for things that are solid, placing thoughts that will be revolved around my fiction and not what truly sits in front of you.

When I encounter different levels of pain because there isn't a focus of strength and revelation, I have to shake my head because the tragedy that I watch develop is being denied access to the future. Whether making a deal that involves financial transactions or simply communicating a secret to your friend, honesty will only bring genuine results for your balance.

Keep it straight folks or continue staying lost in the woods of disaster.

"I am flattered that folks find my words profound, it is very humbling to be identified in a unique category that has been established by simply being myself. I love using my voice to uplift the thoughts of others and trigger the desire to grow #honored"

A.D.Whittington

Praying for love

Finding true love is rare but very important to MOST of us. There is no obligation or requirement to have a mate on the intimate level, but it's mighty nice to get a hug from a warm soul versus a pillow. There is someone reading this right now saying they are perfectly content being alone, but your experiences may be traumatic, scarring you and leaving your defenses up. I get it, I promise I do. There is nothing wrong with understanding the beauty of silence; I am not trying to change your mind, I just need to put a bug in the ear of those who truly desire more.

We live in tough economical times and finding a job is nearly impossible; the same goes for a soul mate. I am not speaking of occasional hanky-panky or a fun date to hang out with on Friday or Saturday night, but something that stays strong because of genuine love. It sounds beautiful and feels even better, but when you have never been embraced and had your heart stroked the right way, will you be able to handle the hurricane of magnificent joy?

I listen to folks complain about what they want in their significant other, stating all the horrible things that have happened in their past. It ranges from mental and emotional abuse to just flat out lying and cheating. Nobody should have to deal with deceitful pain, regardless of what you want in life, so it does matter what happens. I watch these same victims get what they ask for with perfection and then they don't know "how to act" as my grandmother Lucinda Whittington would say. You have to be honest with yourself and learn what you truly mean with these requests. I know it's hard to trust but is it right to make others suffer for things they didn't do? Come on now, that's rude and not something you should be proud of. If you have been missing romance and all the sweet things, why not show appreciation once the ball gets rolling from your brilliant Casanova? Let that woman cook dinner for you and rub your back, she knows you have been working all day and you need to rest, but what do you do? Come in, grab your plate and complain that it wasn't perfect; now you're going out with your boys because you're ticked off at how stupid she is and you continue to tell her that she doesn't "get jack 'ish right." Ughhhh!!!! I am so annoyed with ungratefulness from men and women.

You want so much and can be the perfect this and that to someone, but is that really true? Are you built for a mature relationship based around sincerity? You think I'm tripping, but you should check yourself on what you give out right now and determine if it is in fact your very best for the journey to eternal peace in the romance department. You need to grow and learn yourself, you might soon discover that **YOU** are the problem and need some serious adjusting to even start with better results in life. As they said centuries before my existence "be careful what you ask, you just might get it".

"Sometimes I don't feel like being logical, balanced or available for everybody else's strength. Sometimes I just want to exist and not have to live up to expectations. Sometimes I just don't feel like doing anything at all...at those times I do all of the above and I have peace. Take care of yourself first, without the proper care; nothing else can ever be accomplished successfully.

A.D. Whittington

LOVE FLIGHT 101

With the sun shining bright, so is my spirit. I have spent many days, weeks, months and years observing the actions of other human beings and I've noticed that there is a universal meaning behind certain emotions with the capacity of containing absolutely 'nothing'.

I am slightly disturbed and looking at legitimate reasons for why people place priority on others versus showing respect to their own existence. I have searched high and low for any sign of light concerning negative and warped relationships; platonic or intimate. It really leaves me blank to watch men and women that take care of someone else's needs but they do not have those same desires fulfilled in their personal space. We lack so many values in America and there are individuals that block out reality just so they can say they are connected to another person, regardless of the emotional stress that develops over time.

If you don't know what I'm talking about or never dealt with it first hand, just take a look around and evaluate the true focus of love these days. When you have two people that are supposed to be 'equal' but one is always pushing forward while the other simply reaps the benefits of monetary and emotional giving, there is a slight problem with the balance. Never give more of yourself than the other will even attempt to offer. Stop looking at love with such simple standards; raise them to match what will actually make you happy. **DO NOT**, and I repeat, **DO NOT** give all of your mind, soul and paycheck into a situation where the missing piece for your puzzle to be complete is below your requirement but not fitting naturally. You want to make sure everything you share with others will always return and have the ability to continue recycling with the wonderful things you have thrown into the atmosphere.

In short boys and girls, stop falling crazy in love with someone that doesn't deserve all the splendid things you dish out. Wake up and realize you are being used with no intention from the other person of sharing true love with that fantasy ending. So many of you will deny this or make excuses, constantly trying to justify and defend what is clearly a disaster of the spirit but very bold to the rest of us. It is the ultimate sacrifice to address yourself and answer questions about your lifelong cravings, but it's the first step to learning what truly makes a difference with the final destination in your heart; eternal stability.

Always have sincere intentions.......

Welcome to the Arena of Truth, where balance and peace fight the evil faux pas of the world everyday. Today's match is sponsored by Serenity & Focus and proceeds funded with help from Reality. Today's opponents are squared up and ready to go round for round. The seats are sold out and it looks like the concession stand is open folks, you will need to grab a snack and a cold soda for the highlights. And here they come now~~~>the "Brawler" in all black and trying to stay in stealth mode of deceit, standing at a solid weight of useless substance and still avoiding eye contact with others THE USERRRRRRRRR!!!!!! *Crowd sends a roar of booooooo!!!!!!

And weighing in with finesse and grace with a razor sharp style cutting deep into the zone, rolling in like a freight train A. D. THEEEEEE TRUTHHHHHH WH-III-TTTT-IIII-NNNN-GGGGG-TTTT-OOOO-NNNNNN!!!!! *The crowd goes stupid and starts jumping on tables and chairs. Ok, I did magnify that entrance to show the difference of what everybody embraces, even if you can't see it, it's definitely the path of champions. I did all that hustling for your attention to address a simple topic but super annoying to my mind; people using others in life to get what they want.

I don't have to drag this one out because you

already know what is it. The typical mind can understand you should never be deeply rooted in areas of your life that aren't genuine with a purpose. I watch people cling onto others just because they know that person will do anything for them. The intentions are definitely not to pursue a future; they just give a little bit of shine to false hope for the longing mind. I will never get that part of the thinking because nothing even eats at the heart with the cruel intention. Yeah, that's cruel, you know you don't like that girl in any form of romance or even want to sit in her presence for more than 5 minutes so why are you taking money for a bill or allowing her to purchase items you need? WRONG! And you just said he was annoying but you're getting in the car to go to the mall with him? Wow, ok, I can catch on with your fly style. NOT! Far from that and not something to be respected.

Let me give you a few simple pointers I hope you truly eat well and allow to digest into your spirit. If you take gifts or favors, that opens up a little sun to shine slightly. Even if it's dim, the seed is planted and the lingering begins. It's selfish to hold someone's emotions hostage just because you think you can. They like you but you aren't the ultimate stop of luxury. Search your soul for better balance and truth because currently you are in the column of L-O-S-E-R!!! I don't even care you might not return to this spot, you need to stop reading anyway and evaluate how you're living with your energy for the rest of the world.

The bottom line is, DO NOT connect or even give feedback to someone you have absolutely no interest in growing with on some level (and growing on their shopping list of things to buy you personally does NOT count sir/ma'am). I see you thinking about it and if you never tell anyone out loud, I am glad I touched something in your mind that says, "I get it and I'm changing today".

Make sure you do the right thing

I write things in a manner that anyone can read without feeling repulsed because of inappropriate content, but that doesn't mean I have to talk in circles to avoid hurting people's feelings. When honesty starts to fly from any direction, bullets are definitely going to land in someone's chest and leave a mean scar. My thoughts are simple; some folks need to be touched in their spirit so they can recognize there's another road that their brain needs to take a walk down. I will never understand the world we live in and I stopped trying to rationalize or get my answer a long time ago. If you run around and overdramatize things that aren't real but find a way to soothe other folks that are lost, you are disrupting your spirit and creating tension in your own life.

I refuse to ever go into a shell that keeps me mute on what the real issues are in the same universe all of you exist in. I am a human being that has gone through many experiences and I learned from them ALL. Imagine that, a lesson in living, one of the main ingredients in the recipe for success and growth. Hmmmm, I have to say that's worth some textbook credit.

The views I have are not going to "fix" anyone, they are just thoughts I have on different situations and I pray it can open up the eyes of lost minds and trigger the desire to re-evaluate how that little wheel turns in your attic up there. You won't always agree with what I write, I understand, never asked you too; just asked you to consider the options of receiving possibilities to always head in the right direction. It doesn't matter how you do things when you're pressing forward, just as long as you gave your best and used positive energy to attempt the task; the rest will be fine, even if it turns out wrong. There's this word called mistakes. There is absolutely nothing wrong with failing, but the understanding comes when you decide to turn everything around and learn to win.

I pray my words will be a glow for the discouraged mind and a spark of fire for the stubborn heart; either way, I am going to always use my voice as a megaphone to push what is right according to things I have learned will generate delight.

"I really, really dislike forwards and/or chain text, with no room for improvement in that area. Thanks for your understanding."

A.D. Whittington

PUBLIC SERVICE
ANNOUNCEMENT:

Acknowledge lesbian/gay/bi/transgendered (LGBT) folks you know in public, nobody will think you're weird or suddenly included in the LGBT roster except a population of ignorant human beings that don't matter anyway. If you're with the ignorant section of the stadium, you definitely need to evaluate your existence and purpose because that's the vibe you are involved with.

Don't worry about what people think; if someone is genuinely a good person, there's no need to be embarrassed about interacting with him or her. How rude is that? These are childhood manners and being polite is lacking in our society. For the ladies in the world, if a female in men's clothes walks into the public restroom, please don't look scared, she will not hurt you, she just has to use the same facility you do because you all have the same body parts (where do I come up with these things, I'm a genius). If you see a guy that is feminine and he's carrying a purse, please don't make him uncomfortable by staring at him for ten minutes. What are you trying to accomplish with all that looking? Yes men don't typically have a purse but if that's what he wants to do, your money was not used to make the purchase of that item so it doesn't affect you.

Things that other people do will not always make sense but it doesn't have to, it's not your life. What makes LGBT folks so bad? You weren't sent to earth to change people or tell everyone what needs to be different about their life; you're not on the 'redesign-of-souls' team so stop trying to justify your actions. Treating others with love and respect is one of the basic rules in life, regardless of what someone's personal decisions are. As long as that person is not disrespecting you or causing negative energy to invade your existence, there shouldn't be a strange evaluation to overcome. You don't have to think hard about doing the right thing, just approach each situation with a goal of being fair and you'll be fine.

"You shouldn't have to bash others to get folks on your side or to support you, your wonderful personality should be enough to win votes."

A.D. Whittington

Why can't we all just get along?

There are lots of people that say they want honesty and progression but they avoid the right way to obtain it and keep it (KEYWORD: "keep"). I guess I will never understand the reason for folks not using what they have to assist others. I watch people go to great lengths to try and destroy the character of anyone that intimidates their presence because they are scared of what might happen. It really doesn't matter what other people do, as long as your game is tight and you are investing great energy into your efforts, nobody can beat you. Stop looking over your shoulder to see where the competition is, you are wasting precious time you can invest into your own project to perfect the craft.

I get the picture you're painting and it looks like the colors are running off the canvas. Instead of going against traffic and fighting a very unnecessary battle, why not join forces with your "competition" and make one small thing explosive to the world? I see promoters, artists, career professionals, etc., etc. (you get the point) jump on social networking sites and demolish the character of another person. I listen to people describe someone that is in the same field they are pursuing and the negative comments are humiliating. It leaves me with a blank stare and I can't quite gather the same chains to help assist in the beating. I always run the vision through my brain of how powerful the multiple minds could be together instead of forming thick clouds of poisonous smoke that nobody will respect once the horns have been blown. What is the goal in being so negative? Ohhhh, you're nervous about what you're going to lose because someone else has shown up? Why? Are you not efficient enough by yourself? Is your planning not strong enough to keep you grounded with success? You all should think about it and re-evaluate the approach. I don't play on anyone's team so if I decide to spend time in one arena versus another, it's not personal; it's simply because I wanted to engage in that area. I have loyalty to myself and just because I attend one party doesn't mean I hate the other person that's throwing a party across town; it means I chose to spend my money, which I earned, in a different location.

Attitudes fly because people tend to jump into fires without looking. Take a moment to see what the real issue is and you can work through to the root and actually make mature choices before you look so ridiculous. It doesn't matter who's better, you just focus on being your best. I am not saying everyone will hold hands and get along, that's not realistic, but does there have to be extreme drama each time there is an event, business venture, party or life crisis? If there are several great minds planning separate things, the bottom line is to gain recognition, I get it. Is there that much of a requirement to conduct a mental and spiritual bloodbath just to be a functioning adult? If you are touched by what you're reading, you might need to try another road when traveling in life, it gets a lot better when you do things on a positive note. You can't control everyone but you can put a hold on your own actions. Stay centered with what you do and the rest will be figured out when the time is right. I am not the peacemaker, just someone rooting for the better today.....

Stop being so nosey....

So you want to know the details of the latest gossip? Wow, that's a broad river to cross because privacy is something that should be guarded in society. Although social networks and various sites on the internet will exploit and tell tidbits of intimate tales, is that really what we should consider concrete information?

I know that everything in life can be interesting if given the right intro, but is it a requirement to put your two cents in on EVERYTHING??!!?? Man, I get so irritated when I meet people that are just plain nosey. You know what I'm talking about. The folks who jump on everybody's status updates on the social network site without knowing the details, choosing sides openly to dig a deeper hole for later regret. What about when you see them and the first sentence they part from their lips is in "concern" about situations that don't have anything to do with them? I know we are all guilty of gossip; you have to stay up on things happening in the world, but do that in the privacy of your home with individuals you can trust not to drag the details into the streets.

I get random messages or text all the time asking me about things that are not any of my business, but I have been trusted to hold the information. Do you honestly think I am going to spill the beans on open ground to fill curiosity? I value the position I hold in life of being a solid backbone for men, women, boys and girls in my area that have nobody else to talk to. I pride myself on staying out of the web that tangles the mind into holding stories I will just discard because I refuse to store the components. It is pointless to be wrapped up in the world because it's not even relevant to the daily functions.

What is it about knowing the vast design that makes the world different, on a scale of spicy times two? Will you get a raise at work because you know who is sleeping with who? Oh I forgot, there's a contest that pays $1,000,000,000.00 to the person with the most access to everyone else's personal space. WRONG! There is not a valid reason for anyone to live for things circling in the air; it's just a desire in order to escape your own levels of misfortune. Evaluate the things you are reading right now and be honest. Do a self-cleanse; it takes 5 minutes. If you are that desperate to be wrapped up where you aren't invited, there's a reason to adjust and redirect. If someone does not tell you, there is probably a very strong and definite possibility, THEY DON'T WANT YOU TO KNOW! Stop searching all over for things not intended for you. When there's a fight or an argument on public display, sit there and watch so you can enjoy all you want but why go home and make a million calls updating others; it still equals 'none of your business'. I enjoy the fact I am considered to be a source of NON-information because I don't blast the news of local happenings on Channel 7 and Fox 21. I am content receiving what's meant for me to know and if you choose to exclude me from the circle of hype happenings, I promise I will make it another day breathing free from dramatic blocks in my spirit.

It's not your battle........

The fact that I can create pictures with words is amazing to me when I read the things I paint. I consider the world a blank canvas and thoughts are the colors, you just have to construct a visual with your words so your mental art can be displayed and admired by anyone available to appreciate it. I have talked about this on different occasions so if you have followed my artwork from the beginning, don't yawn with boredom; this is just a refresher to add the new touches of recent positive energy with others.

I always enjoy hitting a nail on the head; it lifts my soul to an open forum of challenges. I talk to people who say they read my personal opinions (and that is all my words are) and they feel like I was talking straight to them. Of course I had no clue I was knocking at his or her door because that would mean I had taken time to reach out to every single person in the world individually and determine what to say. I don't even think twice about things that pop into my brain, I just let the most important topics spring into the air, thus giving all of you something to receive and absorb into your spirit.

The most recent heavy storm to cross my mind is the way we function as a society with being too wrapped up with a loved ones personal life. The troubles that exist can be painful and somewhat devastating, but our job as outsiders is to support and continue love. The point of inserting yourself into the corner pocket for a too-close-for-comfort view drives a tack into the wall so deep, nothing will draw it out. I used so many vocabulary words to simply say, stop taking on the feelings attached to things that have absolutely nothing to do with you directly.

Your friend is fighting with his or her mate but why are you upset? Your "bestie" is ready to fight the dude from down the street and you are going to jump in. Why? The crowd you rode to the club with is approaching a mini riot because somebody in the car with you said they don't like the way everybody at the scene looked at "your peeps"; now you're hyped and grabbing weapons. Why? Do you see how stupid that looks as you read it? For those that are trying to rationalize with the screen, you definitely need to slow your life down and figure out what world you live in and catch the first thing smoking back to your home planet, FAST!!!

Just because someone has anger or hurt emotions, stop jumping in the car of senselessness and take a moment to understand mankind. When folks are upset, they usually react with their irrational and damaged heart, which doesn't always equal logical thinking. When you get the story of their "boo" ticking them off, what started out as an argument about gas has turned into the tale of abuse and betrayal. You fly off the handle and give the "boo" the "side-eye" but when the story is played out, it was simply about a hurt ego and holding insecurity with truth but since you didn't analyze anything, you just immediately joined the irrelevant troop of losers. Yeah, I had to give it to you that raw because that's how silly you act in those pointless moments. I know this doesn't make sense to everyone and of course, there's a genius that can make logic of all the foolishness to their group of small minded followers, but as you journey through life, process the fact that you need to grow, for yourself.

Writer's Block

This is my first book but I have been writing for years and I am so disappointed in individuals that don't display their ability to communicate with words in a positive way. They are everywhere and you all know there is a huge market for negative bloggers. From observation, because I have not actually met any of them, they are truly wasting their skills. You would think that someone with no education or other choices for a future would be the only guilty parties, but the bloggers are usually very smart and college graduates. Some, not all, bloggers write about famous people but have never even been in their presence. Does that stem from jealousy and envy or just a lack of expanding brainpower to create legitimate articles worth reading? It gets attention because the following for these (insert sarcastic tone) "wonderful" writers is huge but it still doesn't make it right. It just shows we live in a society that enjoys the failure of others versus uplifting the right thing. Folks want to enjoy other people's downfalls and pass judgment instead of focusing on their own journey.

I'm not mad, just confused. I watch the same shows, enjoy the same entertainers, process life on the same planet as everyone else but I have yet found the urge to be overjoyed that someone famous is strung out on drugs or found a surrogate to carry their child. Who cares??? Will the above reported information affect their ability to fulfill their contract? How much money will I lose personally because they were kissing their co-star? I read updates on famous people but I can't support lies or assumptions without valid proof. As a nation we have made famous people little fish in a huge aquarium with bright lights shining down. They don't have the opportunity to live life and deal with things in a normal 'I'm-having-a-bad-day-because-I'm-fighting-with-my-wife/husband-because-I'm-a-human-being' type of way; they have to cater to the outside world even when they're not entertaining us. Think about what I'm saying and stop jumping all over the place. I know there is a price for them to pay, but why does it have to cost them their sanity in their private lives? They signed up to make records or movies and people have placed huge expectations on them with just going to the grocery store for milk. That has nothing to do with the concert tickets I bought to go enjoy 3 hours of great preparation.

None of you reading want to keep slaving once you leave that particular work site; you go into a different mode. You might love your job and even take your work home for the weekend, but there is no possible way you don't retreat to some type of privacy and release stress the way you want. There are no cameras in your yard when you run to the car in your pajamas just to find a slip of paper and you don't have to worry about anyone reporting your kids getting suspended for fighting because you're just a normal person. Famous people are just like you, they just have a higher platform based on their job titles. I'm not obsessed with famous people; I'm just obsessed with being fair in life.

"When I hear that people have said negative things about me, I feel sorry for them not getting to know me or appreciating how truly wonderful I am."

A.D.Whittington

Don't form opinions based on 'nothing'.

I **have** been connected with a lot of different personalities and it just added to my focus in the equation of learning more about people. We are all different and we will all have our own story to tell. I am blessed to hold versatility as one of my characteristics but I know how to use it. I am not being fake because I can change according to my surroundings, I just have the ability to observe and react. When I see things that don't match my energy, I simply back away and find the appropriate route for my life. I don't stomp off with anger and refuse to interact with others, there are too many options I can choose in life and nobody forces me to remain stuck anywhere. I don't have to round up troops to fight a deadly war; nothing is that serious in life. I don't throw a tantrum because I can't get my way and attempt to make everyone identical to what I have grown to be, I simply respect the choices of other human beings in the free world.

Why must we as a nation have issues with someone because they are different? That's the ignorance that takes over on a regular basis. I hear folks say they don't like someone and after my mental scan of the details, it boils down to the fact that they don't like that person because they don't understand or agree with the way that person lives. It sounds stupid huh? I know, it will never make sense to me either. I have learned how to focus on the important values in life and make my choice based on substance. I will not dislike someone because my friend doesn't like him or her. I am determined to open the eyes and ears of closed souls everywhere, not because I want robots patterned after me but because it's time to bring reality to the list of priorities. If you don't want to stop and evaluate your own place on your timeline of growth, you have no right to ever have an opinion about others.

I like some people more than others; some I don't like at all. That is the thought I had one morning that triggered this approach for the light. That might sound rude but there is absolutely nothing wrong with those being the feelings of anybody. Just because you don't like something another person says or does in life, it doesn't make it wrong. You just don't like it and who are you again? Riiiigggghhhhttttt, you have not been deemed the authority to stamp your thoughts everywhere. Who cares if they dress weird according to you, that doesn't mean they aren't intelligent and strong. They might be searching for a unique way of expression, definite signs of a person having a mind of their own. When I see that, I am intrigued and drawn like a magnet. Some people may be negative behind the entire glow, but how will you ever know if you don't connect directly?

I get so detached when I watch how society places tags on situations and people without thorough research of what all of it really means. I'm not saying you have to walk up to every stranger you see and start a conversation, stop being dramatic, but you do have to reserve your opinions of negative response until you have. This is something I will be passionate about for the rest of my life and I will always point an arrow toward. I don't care if I'm repeating myself, it burns me up and I have to use my voice to speak up for the right way in life. I am licensed on reality, I have been living it for over 30 years and it only gets better for me each day. Yep, I am all for treating others right. Yep, I am rooting for people to slow their brains down and give others a fair chance and stop forming barriers based on what others say; you don't know why the feelings are that way and what the history is. Yep, I am going to hold my head up high when I defend the shy kid in the room because all the other idiots are too shallow to walk over and have a conversation. He's shy, why would he just walk over and jump in the circle, taking a risk of being rejected? Come on y'all, we have to do better. Life is too short to sit around being negative when in reality; the real reason isn't even valid. Based on all the experiences I have had in life mixed with the general feedback from people that are grounded and logical, I have arrived at the places I write about. I can't jump in your car just because I like you and you dress nice or have a lot of money because when you opened your mouth to communicate verbally, I learned you have a lot of stupidity. We must fight for doing the right thing, even when the majority decides not to. You all know the difference between good and bad, the secret isn't locked away in some cave under the ground. I am sending out positive energy and focus for someone that is here to gain a better connection with his or her inner weakness and I have faith in your desire to make the step for yourself.

Dear Social Networking Site:

I'm writing to you on behalf of all the cowards and people seeking attention. We love the fact you exist because we don't have to deal with real life, we simply post our "vulnerable" (not really, we just want pity points) emotions for the whole world to view and hope it wins us sympathy. Until you were around, we were forced to accept things that are real and actually talk through pain to reach resolution. I know the 'LIKE' button on our favorite social site makes us feel glorified and justified, even when we're wrong, but it's ok, we don't want to be told the right way to do things, we simply want to be uplifted just as we are. I praise you for the space you provide, it is so much better than reality when we face problems in our daily life. We would much rather embarrass ourselves by having fights or humiliating others so our inner-5-year-old can feel like there's been a mission accomplished. Please take this public token of gratitude as our most sincere thanks for giving light on this dark path that was dim (and still is) until you came along. We hail you and will continue to make you feel worthy of all our secrets;

you are, after all, the best place to hold our thoughts...too bad what we write on your canvas has open access and EVERYBODY can look in to give their irrelevant opinions, even when they don't know the full story. We are aware that folks have weak minds and jump on petty trains to just go with what we say; not requiring any research on their own so they can be fair & correct us if needed~~~> THAT'S WHY WE LOVE THIS PLACE. With those types of credentials, we will use you for the wrong things forever and deal with finding peace NEVER. Be proud, we are.

Love,
Folks with no ambition for mental/spiritual growth

P.S. I really like what you've done with the place, no limit on characters when typing; classic :)"

Stop telling all your business online.

Mannnnn, I am going to bruise some toes with this section and I'm very comfortable with that. My mind was stirring and debating on the presentation of what I feel right now. Conclusion: DO IT!!! I am not full of drama and negative controversy, but I do like addressing controversial things that could make a difference. I just made that whole paragraph intro kind of controversial, but I had to let it flow. Just getting myself prepared to tick folks off because what I feel right now will probably apply to half my readers or at least someone you know. I analyzed last night that this post will give me 2 degrees of separation with everyone in the world, guaranteed!

So I wrote about people being nosey, and I even touched on the world feeding off what media prints about celebrities, but I need you to read this in the bathroom so you see yourself in the mirror when it's over. I'm not giving this as an apology for hurting your feelings; I just tend to match the level of drama I am going to unload into your brain. I listen to folks complain about everybody being in their business or always "hating" on them and the first thing I do is evaluate their pattern of living or lifestyle they lead; and I'm not referring to being gay or straight with that reference to lifestyle people. You tired of being talked about? Stop posting so much personal insight on your Facebook, Twitter or anywhere that has a browser address.

I know I don't live with you, so when you're fighting with your "boo", I see it on Facebook and smh ('shake my head' for those who need assistance with the acronyms of the world today. Don't feel bad; I have a teenager on deck for help with all the new phrases because there are bunches). Then you post a status update warning everybody to stop hating on the love you have. Well last week you said you hated this person, announced you were blocking them from your page and now there's a profile picture of the two of you together? I mean really??? Ok, I can clearly see the level of privacy you provide for issues in your personal space; the relationship status jumped from single to in a relationship to it's complicated and now you're married, all in a 2 week period??? Wow, you post about everything else, why didn't we read about the wedding and the way you're playing with the true facts of life? Living together doesn't make you married, it just means you help with the bills and you SHOULD start planning to do some nuptials the right way!!! Real gangsta boo on ya because you are living in a world filled with 20" rims and booming sound systems floating you to the carousel at every town fair. The 'ish is bogus and I am tired of witnessing the foolery (gotta capture every word that is not even listed in the dictionary on this one, it goes with the theme of ignorant elaboration). And what does 'it's complicated' mean anyway? I know it goes right up there with good ol' respectful 'open relationship' which just puts a bow on top of love, but if anything gets "complicated" to me, I tend to stop doing it. I definitely don't want to deal with my emotions connected to another person's heart and have further complications with focusing on the meaning of a concrete and solid forever. I just laughed so hard inside while I was typing, literally and I don't care that you're ticked off or talking junk about me, just make sure you let folks know I said something you don't like and tell them exactly what it is I said. Unless they are stuck in the dusty cave of lost reality with you, they will LOVE what I wrote and completely agree.

And why are you fighting with other people on the internet? I just saw both of you in the same spot but there was silence. I'm not gonna walk up to either of you and say something that might trigger the adult thing to do like verbally COMMUNICATE, but can one of you please throw a punch? I'm definitely not promoting violence, but I mean, that's the level of disgrace you put on your wall, their wall, in a note, uploaded to UStream with a link, sent out in mass text form to mutual friends and reported to the 7:00 news. It was broadcast EVERYWHERE! If anybody is a mutual friend with both of you, they can just pull up a chair and be entertained. It is the most coward form of communication, posting on the web instead of talking. Let's just call you a keyboard thug that has a courageous soul of invisibility. Trying to embarrass someone or make them feel bad doesn't show you're bold and someone to fear, it shows how truly ignorant you are and you don't really have many options to fight a battle that will require extra brain cells.

Oh boy, I have done it now and everybody I have interacted with thinks they are my target, but I don't want you to flatter yourself, you're not that important dear, I am giving a general view agreed upon by many and this directs toward way more than just you. See, you're being arrogant right now and ready to fight. Good, just do it quietly, I actually use my brain to fight, hurts much more than some stupid post or a fist fight. Honesty hurts, but as my grandparents (Gus and Lucinda Whittington-R.I.P.) would say "you'll be fine after the swelling goes down"; your pride is slightly bruised but it might be time to stop running into the wall. I get that folks tick you off and make your blood boil, but does it have to shown through all these words and bad grammar? Yes, I am touching everywhere, if it's going to be confronted, I might as well make everybody mad at once. The words you type aren't even right and since you are the main attraction of Facebook or the social site due to your outrage, write the right thing (see how I used two words that sound alike in the right context? Just that simple). I am not a professor or English major, no formal training in the field of education, but I use my mind to read things and see if it even sounds right. Is the thought being displayed correctly for understanding? Simple technique people, and it's free, just Google the word dictionary and take your pick from several versions.

You already look a mess putting things out there in the first place, don't say "their is a time and spot to meet you so I can beat yo a--". Look at that! It is ridiculous isn't it? The word should be *'there'* for that particular sentence, I just wanted to be extreme for my example. Did you even look at the sentence before you hit 'Share' or 'Post'? I am definitely not trying to say you have to be some genius to write things, but the basics are very easy to follow. Stop typing so much if you KNOW you can't spell (don't play me, you know that's been an issue for you for quite a while now), they have help, just look on the same internet you're using to start a war or tell everybody you used the bathroom; you all about know the play by play post to document movement from one room to another. Get twitter for that and even your followers don't want to know about your detailed love affair and cleaning up afterwards. Be considerate to others. I know it's your choice to post what you want, I know I do, but why don't you have more respect for yourself? It makes sense to tell everyone you're pregnant or just got engaged but do we have to hear it with EVERY single post, tagged on the end or incorporated somehow with stumping your toe? Oh, someone posted about his or her new dog and you just found relevance to that by saying congrats and adding your great news of getting married (which technically you're not because you guys just started living together two days ago, remember???). Nobody asked you that and it had nothing to do with karate, Charlie (that's how irrelevant it is, just like I showed with that last sentence; useless). The box says 'What's on your mind?' and I am all about expression, but if the ONLY thing on your mind is that ring or your booski, you need some hobbies. And then in 6 months when you break up, the embarrassment will crowd you. Ohhhhh, you're saying you're not embarrassed, but you wanted it to be etched in stone about how in love you are and how after 2 weeks you discovered this to be the one like no other, but clearly it's identical to every other relationship you had; dissolved and fizzled away. Single? Oh wow, not you. It was perfect, your Facebook and photos told us that. Or were you trying to convince yourself? Hmmmmmmm, that was a good one.

I'm writing a lot with this topic because I have A LOT to say; clearly. I am going to shoot the truth about everything that annoys everyone concerning online networking. I don't even have to write another section for this one, it's being played out as the folks it irritates reads this. Do you not realize people know you outside the internet? If you're not on someone's friends list, I guarantee someone you're not personally connected to still knows you. That profile picture of a Porsche SHOULD be your Honda. I'm not talking bad about what you drive, but can you just tell the truth? I saw you at McDonald's bagging orders but you have a spread of $100 bills across your face showing 10 pair of Jordans in a house that isn't even located in the same town. Unless McDonald's is stacking some gold plated fries, that's not yours!!! Oh it is??? MY BAD!!! So now you're letting everyone know you are involved with illegal activity, not to mention the picture of you rolling a blunt and making rings with the smoke. You are not invincible but you post that somebody snitched on you. I am not even going to ask are you serious because you just loaded my home page/live feed with your tantrum about wanting people to stop being jealous and get a life. I know I'm not jealous of someone with pending jail time because it's documented you carry a gun and shoot anyone that looks at you funny or that you don't want to talk. What does someone 'looking at you sideways' even look like??? The reality in all of this is, you choose what you want others to know. And NO, I'm not a snitch, they couldn't pay me enough to stalk your life and be bored with your nothingness; just giving you some thought provoking words to help you on this journey and I pray it motivates you to do something productive with your life, or lack of.....

What's your addiction?

So I am extremely random with this one. I had to start putting the words down as soon as I parted my eyes this morning, something was jumping out of my chest. I live for the fire to roar in the form of words, I am so addicted to speaking what's on my mind and I certainly have the tools to do so. I have accepted that I have an addictive personality and dive in deep with interest for things I like.

I used to be addicted to Farmville, the popular game on Facebook that held my attention for hours, rolling into days on end. And let's not forget my addiction to ironing, despising wrinkles on sight. I know these sound silly to you, but I know what goes on in my head and I have no shame revealing the core facts. I tend to be from one extreme to the other and things in life just fall on the see saw where they fit appropriately. When I am really digging something and find a connection, it's all or nothing. I don't swing in the gray area but I'm not saying that's healthy, sometimes it would make things less stressful for me because I hang in black or white with the majority of activities, situations or people I deal with.

You might not have a crazy 'addiction-to-the-bone' as I do, but if there is a chance that you cling to your heart's desires without determining any outside points of reference, it's time to truly look at what damage might happen if the wrong focus is given to the wrong priority. I was addicted to Farmville and that's just what it was. I set my alarm to harvest crops and animals; getting annoyed when my farm wasn't respected. It's harmless, I know, but once I went on my farm, I was stuck for hours and didn't know how to be an adult and push away from the virtual world I had thrown myself into. I was recruiting everyone I knew to be my neighbor and I became offended if they declined or made comments implying Farmville was stupid or juvenile. Yeah, I had it bad. Notice I said 'had', past tense. It is just a game but it became my world because I was addicted. I was addicted to Facebook games period but Farmville was the baby of my heart. Awwwwww, that's so sweet. NOT! I had to shake myself and slow down the irrelevant patterns so I could redirect into the tunnel of realistic success.

Nobody can judge you on what makes your blood pump, that's what makes you smile and you have to dash into a mode of balance for yourself. I am not going to preach to you about things that aren't my business, I am just going to advise you to evaluate where you exist in your heart and your mind; make sure you are addicted to things that will keep you going toward the light of everlasting growth. I must admit I miss my farm, but my addiction to writing is much more promising and I think the real coins I gain from this harvest will allow me to become more than a cartoon character walking around to collect dreams going nowhere for my personal journey.

Sorry to all the loyal farmers that still take pride in their work, I just had to leave that road because I was getting absolutely NO results with my hard work on the screen. I support your loyal efforts; I just fell back so I could move forward. Thanks for your understanding, please don't call me a trader. This message is approved for all Farmvillians everywhere

Letting go is healthy....

I have learned to address life with an open mind and I consider all areas a lesson to be gained as a blessing. I know I am supposed to be giving the full details of my past to help you understand my journey into the future but I can never stop praising the works of God.

Once upon a time, I had a job that was sufficient for my basic needs. I wasn't making millions but I can't complain because everyday the light switch turned on and I had water to wash my body. The refrigerator had an abundance of joy for my stomach and I was able to drive in a vehicle instead of walk where I needed to go. The simple joys of life could be embraced with great shielding of a freedom, living without distress. I was in a job description that I absolutely love, working with people and fulfilling joy in their heart. I woke up over a year ago to go into work and near the end of my shift; I was told it was my last day. I was laid off for budget cuts and my mind simply took the words to mean, my time at this stop is up. I could have been devastated and broken or walked in a cloud not able to see my hand in front of my face. I could have racked my brain about the real reason they laid me off and not someone else; was it truly budget cuts? I could have even cried in fury and panic because I have a family to feed and it's not great timing, but those were not the reactions my mind absorbed.

I have gone through so many haystacks and pine needles with my world but I refuse to allow things not going how I anticipate or want them to go to destroy my drive forward. I learned a long time ago we are all headed toward our goal, and depending on what you pray about, the prep is different. If you ask for more money but can't manage what you have, God knows you won't be able to handle it. If you always complain about wanting a new car but never take care of the one you have then He would be wasting His time giving you the full desires and you do not appreciate the basics things you have now that keep you going. We all have a responsibility to our inner self; make sure we become healthier with every moment of struggle and beyond. I used to be irresponsible with my thinking and much more destructive with my actions. I wouldn't give my all when He looked out for me and made sure I was okay in areas of finance and stability. He allowed me to suffer with quite a few things in my life and it opened my eyes to the power of what my mind controls. I spent quite a while at the place I received pay and truly gave my best. I didn't steal from the company or create situations built around drama. I remained focused and did all I could to be positive for the outside, remaining in the flow of representing as my Father taught me to do in society. I received the news and I just sat with a weird peace of closure because I knew that I was in no fault of the decision, I gave a grand performance as instructed from my Daddy (Jesus) when I started this journey.

I believe strongly that life is like laundry and wardrobe; you have to mix the clean and dirty in two separate piles to distinguish the difference. A lot of times we ask for clean clothes to be placed on the pile but dirty underwear and socks are still holding old odors that will crawl into the fresh aroma. God has to nudge us sometimes and I know that when we don't let go of things that can't share the same space as the new task, it must be removed without an option. I am not sad or frustrated. I don't feel the need to cry or be angry. I haven't reached my multi- million-dollar destiny but I do know that my heart is settled and open, no obstacles or dirty laundry to stop the process.

"Set the tone for how you want people to treat you"

A.D.Whittington

Your past is your future victory....

I want to give you some advice as you read and nothing short of reality; make the moments of struggle go toward your good. There is no way for you to ever accomplish complete joy if you don't start by taking out the trash resting comfortably in your heart and spirit.

It's time to let go of some things and replace the spot they once held with beautiful songs you write yourself. I am not taking you too fast; I am simply giving you the challenge of making the times that hold you hostage a stairway to glory. I am going to tell you, I have buried several hatchets that used to chop at my spirit. I endured abuse in younger years and had horrible experiences with abandonment, but I had to release the thoughts because I could not move forward and live a fruitful life.

I am not criticizing you for dealing with certain things that hurt but I am giving you some words to push you into the cyclone so the bad vibes can go ahead and sting, only to heal properly down the road. I had to forgive my abusers in my heart, so it wasn't lingering in my mind. I used to cry all the time because I wasn't accepted in life and nobody understood my hidden pain or even cared to notice. I was confused about why my biological father didn't ever want to deal with me or why he didn't show me love; consistently denying my existence as a human being, much less recognizing me as his daughter. He still is not connected with me, but I really could care less at this point of my growth, it's his loss and that definitely is not an emotion I can waste on that chapter of my life. I used to wonder why, among so many other things, I could never keep a relationship or friendship for extended periods of time; running in and out of people's arms and ultimately their bed. Yeah, I am doing 'Media Takeout: Scandal Edition' on myself in this section, not much anyone can slander about my past, I speak up for things I did because it molded me into this wonderful person that has grounded understanding of all personality types. Am I proud or am I bragging? Of course not, just being real, as I feel the world should do to advance in spaces on the board. You don't have to write a book or expose all your embarrassing moments, but you do have to confront these things with yourself.

"I know the struggles you face might discourage your pursuit of success but fighting only makes you stronger & prepared for anything."

A.D. Whittington

The Beginning....
of your new outlook.

Acknowledgements:

So this is the part of the book that definitely has no format or order. I have to address the folks that have been profound in my life and remained consistent. I can't recognize every single person that I like or that has been nice to me, I would need another book for that; I just have to shine light on the folks that made an impact with things they have done on my journey.

I have to be honest, it took me forever to write this part, I just didn't want to sit down and have to think. You all probably think I'm a genius with words after reading this book but I have my flaws and procrastination can be one of them.

Let's start at the top of the chain and work our way through. I can't continue without recognizing God, He has always seen my precious existence and prepared me to do great things from the beginning. I cry each time I think bout Him protecting me from harm and never leaving my side. Though there was pain, there was always a final vision and He knew I would be an asset for the message the world needs to hear. I will forever be a warrior for Him; He has proven to me that even when I stumble, I will recover with a renewed look at the journey and fight for the drive forward.

I must acknowledge my son, Jamison Lewis. I am glad I am your mother and thank you for accepting my love into your life. I know your road can be hard, teenage years are difficult for everyone, but with hard work, you are pushing past the odds. Thank you for encouraging me to be my best, as a writer but more importantly as your parent. We have a very unique bond and that can never be taken away, God has blessed this union and I know you are destined to do great things. I embrace the experience and look forward to the rest of our life together.

I will always hold the highest level of respect for Lucinda McKinley Whittington. She's my maternal grandmother and that lady was amazing when she lived here on earth. Lucinda or "Mother" was the first person to ever accept me for who I am. I revealed secrets early about myself and she simply assured me that no matter what I do in life, I was still a great person that should strive to do wonderful things in the world. Through the years, long before she developed health issues, I could confide in her and trust her thoughts with directions I should take. She never stuck her nose in my business but she never had a problem being honest if I asked for her feedback. Mother never judged things I did and she always treated me like I was her granddaughter; pushing me to seek happiness, even when others close to me ridiculed and degraded me. I love you Mother and I'm honored you were involved in this finished product.

Gus Whittington or 'Daddy' was Lucinda's husband and he was the first father figure I ever encountered in life before God took him home. He taught all of us about love for one another and what a man should do to take care of his family. He didn't believe in physical discipline but he did believe in raising us the right way with morals and values, providing much more than a roof over our head. We share the same birthday and I was in love with the man that always nurtured me and cared for me, doing things outside of 'food on the table'. A lot of men in the world think financial support is the only thing a child needs but affection and quality time are what build character. No other man showed me a smile simply because I existed and Daddy made me cherish what a real man should always be.

Tanea Whittington, you might be shocked to see your name in this section because we don't talk every week but I have to say thank you. You never closed your heart to me and you always showed me that you were proud of me. I always said first cousins are just a parent away from being a sibling and that's how I feel about you. The talks we have had over the years when I was caught in confusion and had nowhere to turn meant a lot and helped groom me toward this success. From checking on me during those times to visits in my adult years, it all will forever mean something profound and special to me. Even though none of the above was a big deal to you, I know you did everything because you love me.

I happened upon some great and wonderful people in the past six years of my life and the impact they have had is tremendous. I can't put a value on my life but I can put a value on what the folks mean to it with the simplest gestures. I am very big on whom I actually trust, no matter how much I like you and think you're cool, can I be myself and rely on you? Do you care about my well-being and things I am attempting to pursue? Are my goals important to you even if you don't understand them or agree? I don't need a bunch of people that always tell me what I WANT to hear, I keep folks close to me that are honest with me but respect me and my assignment. If you see someone in my personal space on a regular basis, you can trust that they are balanced and headed in the right direction because I am responsible for keeping my world clear of negative energy and bonds that can be easily broken. Yeah, I'm something serious to deal with, I require the minimum on maintenance but I do require folks that are content with me outside of my knowledge. People I want to acknowledge have played different roles for me, but it has been significant to my overall development, whether they realize it or not.

Ms. LeKiya Wright, you have been in my life for several years and the day you met me, you expressed that you would always be my friend, regardless of other connections existing. You have stayed true to your word, never changing or making me feel out of place. I've had to crash on your couch or confide in you about mutual situations and you have never betrayed me or left me out when you recognize important people in your life. I can go months without talking to you and when we reunite, it's like we never missed a day. Thank you so much Kiya, I love the value you have added to my life and the genuine love you always make me feel. You're not just my friend under conditions; you are my friend because the connection is meant.

Niss, Niss, Niss Jones....what can I say Lula Bell? I know it it's our nature to fight with each other (hence the name Lula Bell for the old lady and she calls me April Louise) so I can't be but so nice here, lol. I reallllly appreciate everything you have EVER done for me, even before I moved to your town. When I would visit, you always babysat Jamison so I could have free time and once I moved, you allowed me to stay in your home until I found a job and my own place. You never asked me for a dime and we were always a family with everything we needed. We figured out our meals and whatever else had to be supplied for the household to operate smoothly. You are the best....that's the last time I'll ever say anything sweet to you so cherish it, lol.

(I know these acknowledgements might seem lengthy but if you were being recognized, you would appreciate every word....now back to the program).

Sheila Rogers, you are one of the best cooks in America and I appreciate you always feeding me since I can be greedy sometimes, lol. Making some of my favorite dishes to satisfy my appetite and caring about the welfare of my son. You probably didn't realize I paid attention to the little things, but it has made a difference in my life. I know that if I am going to visit you, I will feel welcome and you always treat me with respect. My son has been misunderstood in his life but you always helped me to see the brighter side of his existence. He loves you to death and speaks of how wonderful you treat him when I'm not around. It's hard to find folks you can trust your children with but when it's natural, you must embrace the blessing. Thank you so much for everything!!!!!

I met a young lady through a friend of mine years ago and without knowing any details about me she assisted me with the first project I ever attempted. If anyone knows my history, you know I keep moving and I don't stop. If I realize something isn't working, I don't just quit, I leave it alone to avoid wasting energy and I look for other avenues to follow on the road toward my goal. Tracy Hill, you have been a support for ANYTHING I try, without asking questions. When I attempted to do an internet radio show, you walked me through the whole process and listened to EVERY show, commenting and interacting to let me know you were sincere. When I finished my blog site, you made sure I knew you were reading every word. No matter what I strive for, you have made a difference with your presence and genuine words to push me through to the next stop. I didn't realize how much that meant to me but it definitely made an impact on my drive. Thank you!!!!!

I am not the type of person that believes in giving the title 'BEST FRIEND' to anyone, I don't care how close I get to an individual. I hold a fear of betrayal and eventual destruction of the connection, based on all my experiences with others in life and realizing that most people don't cherish that title to the fullest. I never met anyone that I felt could ever meet my personal standards of what BEST FRIEND meant until I encountered a young lady named Lanette 'Lyn/Shorty Pimp' Hayes. We were total opposites, from personal appearance to style of thinking, but she always made me feel secure about her love for me. I never met someone so loyal, even when I wasn't around, and her existence was so profound that I grew to NEED her in my life. Because of my hesitation with using the term 'BEST FRIEND', even though she proved to be perfect for the role, Lyn was referred to as my 'LOVEBUTTON' since we were so inseparable and plain goofy together. It feels good to be connected with someone you know will never hurt you, even when opportunities are there for them to destroy you. She was taken away from my life and the world on Sept. 17, 2011 but her spirit lives on in the most powerful way. I love you Lyn, you're still very much involved with my growth.

I am beyond fortunate to still have someone in my life that lives in the same pattern of commitment. I was blessed with you Amber Anderson years ago and our unique relationship just keeps getting stronger each day. I appreciate your wisdom and natural ability to maintain stability in my heart, always providing comfort for my basic needs. You don't have an expectation of how I am supposed to be, you just love me the way I am. I can be complex to handle on an intimate level when it comes to friendship but our bond is grounded deeply in sincere emotions. I love you Amber and I am so happy God allowed me to experience how wonderful you truly are.

I will always have a special place in my heart for Latoya Warren, someone that has been around for many years. 'Toya Woya' as I call you because I'm not always mature, you have been there for me in so many ways. From the days of Myspace when we stalked profiles together, there will never be a period of time I won't refer to you as my most dear and true friend. I need you to know that every moment we have shared means something to me, even when you talked bad about me wearing shorts that came above my knees, lol. We have created fond memories and I value the blessing of our connection. I love you!

To my current House of Alexander family (Tanika, Lyn, Jamal, Shavario, Shemese, Kino, Tailika, Trey, Keith, Amber), thank you all for loving and supporting me, we always have a good time together. I appreciate you allowing me to be in your presence; never judging me but always showing respect for the position I hold in each of your lives. We have lost several members over the years but I salute the strength you all have displayed by sticking by my side through any storm. I will admit it's hard to be an Alexander because you have to possess integrity and a will to overcome all negative things with an understanding of what you know truly exist in life, but each of you exceeds the expectation. I pray we continue to grow as a family; remaining unbreakable as a unit, I love you!

From the first day I met Reya and Kenny Talley, you all have treated me like I'm your daughter. Whether it is a listening ear or buying me brakes and changing them in your driveway, you all have me spoiled rotten!!! I appreciate the fact that you don't have an expectation of me, you adore me as I am. I need you to know that the little things have impacted me in a major way, though you have done everything from a genuine place. I am so thankful you all remain an instrumental part of my life and I look forward to sharing my success with you. I love you!

I must definitely acknowledge everyone that has ever abandoned or rejected me; causing me pain. I appreciate each tear I have cried because it pushed me to become stronger for this journey. Those who didn't believe in me and those that never took time to cherish me, those experiences have forced me to always strive for excellence and never ignore my own efforts. God along with you all have been the motivation required and the world thanks you. I love you!

SPECIAL THANKS:

Ms. Tanika Jones, you are truly rare and I am going to try and express my gratitude in this small area. You came into my life almost six years ago and our friendship can never be fully explained with simple words. What we share is much deeper than basic interaction; we always push each other to be better in all areas. You saw something special in me and never let me stop driving forward, always supporting every venture and encouraging me to do work God has intended for me to complete. When I started this project, 'It's My Fault', my list was short of individuals I revealed the details to; you listened to me talk when I didn't even have anything to say. This task has been time consuming but you were available to assist with editing whenever I needed your full attention. I appreciate you accepting the role of being my manager, not because we have a special bond but because you earned it. You have shown me that I can trust you with every aspect of my life; you're outspoken for what's right in life and you always have my best interest at heart. I know you will never betray what I hold in my heart for you and you appreciate things in life that make the road better. You are an important factor for this project and your diligent work has been noticed. I love you!!!!

Lola Brooks, I want to thank you for always being there when I need you most; you're like a mother to me and when I started this journey, you immediately assisted. You give unconditionally and always make sure I'm safe and secure in my personal space; Jamison and I will forever love and appreciate your presence in our lives. Words are hard to find when trying to extend heartfelt emotions toward someone that appreciates you and does everything they can to show that. If you ever wonder about your role on this earth, just read these words and be assured it is required and so many people benefit from your generous heart and giving spirit. I love you!!!!

Jamal Williams, sir, you are amazing. When I started this project, you were available for anything I needed with design along with creative ideas to ensure everything came together with a professional finish. I am forever grateful for the hard work and dedication you invested because of the true love you have for me as a person. I am extremely pleased to have you on my team as Creative Director, there's no other person that can capture my visions exactly as I need them displayed. You have earned your spot in my life, always being a true friend to me; thanks for the long talks about intimate pains as well as overwhelming joy. The journey is far from over and I am excited you will continue right here in the car with me. I love you!

Keith Dorrah, you have no clue how much you mean to my life. From the moment we met, you expressed that you were sent from God to exist in my world. I'll always appreciate everything we have shared and I love how well you know me, inside and out. I don't have a high tolerance for many people but I never seem to get tired of you, for days and weeks on end. I don't respect people that don't respect themselves and I hold you in a high bracket Mr. Dorrah; you never pretend to be something you're not in my presence. I wouldn't change a thing about you; it works perfect with everything that makes me flow. I want to thank you for becoming my personal assistant, even though you have been organizing my life long before this opportunity presented itself. I love the way God had this all lined up and ready to go when He fired the gun at the starting line, lol. I love you!!!

Last but certainly not least, I want to introduce the world to my public relations coordinator, Ms. Tamara Simpson. Tam, you have always been available for professional guidance, your MBA in Business Administration qualifies you to perform all task thrown your way. There's something about your mere existence that draws folks close, giving them an ease of knowing that if you agree with what is going on, it must be good to go, lol. I know you're going to kill me for that last sentence because you're somewhat shy, but it's the truth; you do no wrong. I'm sure you have your flaws but I witness you make it a practice of doing the right thing by others. You are naturally thorough with EVERYTHING and I appreciate your insight on this project. I know I held you hostage seeking your advice but it has paid off for my results. I can't deny you are good at being you and I am beyond honored you are a member of this team. I love you!